# The Lutheran Handbook on Marriage

## About "Winking Luther" and "Katie Lu"

Ever since Martin Luther and Katharina von Bora renounced their vows of celibacy and embraced marriage as a lifelong vocation, Lutherans the world over have accepted marriage as a holy calling, as holy (and sometimes as ascetic) as any religious order or office.

The wry winks and knowing smiles on our forebears' faces indicate, in that oh-so-Lutheran way, that Christ-centered marriage cannot be enjoyed without a well-developed sense of humor. Thanks to some hard work and down-to-earth theology (and maybe a little helpful advice from time to time), Lutheran marriages will continue to exemplify the shared promise of salvation by grace through faith that makes us one.

# The Lutheran Handbook on Marriage

Augsburg Fortress

Minneapolis

THE LUTHERAN HANDBOOK ON MARRIAGE

New brand development editor: Kristofer Skrade
Editors: Gloria E. Bengtson, Laurie J. Hanson
Cover designer: Diana Running
Production editors: Linnea Fitzpatrick, Jessica Puckett, and James Satter
Interior illustrator: Brenda Brown

Contributing writers: Paul J. Blom, Herbert Brokering, Eric Burtness,
Linda Post Bushkovsky, Lou Carlozo, James M. Childs Jr., Eileen Z. Engebretson,
Peder M. Engebretson, Robert Buckley Farlee, Paul N. Hanson, Susan L. Houglum,
Diane L. Jacobson, Rolf A. Jacobson, Susan M. Lang, Kirk T. Livingston,
Catherine Malotky, Jonathan Rundman, Mitzie Spencer Schafer,
Theodore W. Schroeder, Megan Torgerson, Thomas L. Weitzel, Hans Wiersma,
and Barbara S. Wilson

ISBN-13: 978-0-8066-5294-8
ISBN-10: 0-8066-5294-2

10   09   08   07   06                    1  2  3  4  5  6  7  8  9  10

# CONTENTS

## The Lutheran Model for Marriage and Its Biblical Forerunners

## Dating & Courtship

## The Wedding

## The First Year

## Early Years

## Middle Years

## Later Years

## Money, Sex, & Other Fractious Issues

# THIS BOOK BELONGS TO

*Name* _____

*E-mail* _____

*Telephone* _____


*Birth date* _____

*Baptismal birth date* _____

*First communion* _____

*Confirmation date* _____


*Wedding date* _____

*Wedding location* _____

*Members of our bridal party* _____

_____

_____

_____

_____


*My favorite memory from our wedding:*

# ABOUT MY SPOUSE

*Name* _____

*E-mail* _____

*Telephone* _____


*Birth date* _____

*Baptismal birth date* _____

*First communion* _____

*Confirmation date* _____


*My spouse's favorite memory from our wedding:*


*Churches we have belonged to:*

# PREFACE

Fewer institutions are richer with humor and opportunities to laugh (and be laughed at!) than marriage, unless you're counting the institutional church, in which case you're in the wrong book. The joining of man and woman into "one flesh," as Jesus calls it, and the interesting situations that arise from it have made the careers and fortunes of countless cartoonists, stand-up comics, and quack therapists in every culture and on every continent. Well, we want to cash in on a little of that action.

But more importantly we felt called to do this book because marriage jokes never get old, but also because people navigating their way through the tough work of marriage need handy helpful information. Putting those jokes and that information together seemed like a good idea. You be the judge.

The information contained herein is time-tested stuff, written by experts on the Lutheran marriage perspective, which is very peculiar...in a good way. Lutheran couples fortunate enough to endure many decades together all seem to bear certain marks. They're the marks of resilience etched under the grand covenant of baptism and forged in the iron of God's enduring grace. They're the marks of survival where the wrinkles around the eyes reveal both lots of smiling and lots of tears. Our hope is that this book bears those marks as well.

Well, not the tears part quite so much as the smiling.

—KRISTOFER SKRADE

# The Lutheran Model for Marriage and Its Biblical Forerunners

# FIVE IMPORTANT STAGES OF THE LUTHER/VON BORA RELATIONSHIP

**❶ Katharina von Bora escapes from her convent and arrives in Wittenberg.**

In the spring of 1523, several escaped nuns arrived in Wittenberg. Most of them were soon matched with suitable husbands. A match between Katharina von Bora and a Wittenberg student fell through because the young man's parents did not want their son to marry a former nun.

**❷ Martin Luther marries Katharina von Bora.**

In 1525, Martin Luther was one of the few monks in Wittenberg who had not yet married. Some thought it curious that the one who so enthusiastically advocated for the marriage of priests had not himself married. This changed in June, when Martin and Katharina became husband and wife. Each year in June, the Luther-von Bora nuptials are celebrated in Wittenberg.

**❸ Hans Luther is born.**

According to a medieval legend, the union between a monk and a nun could produce monstrous results, including two-headed children! Such an outcome was not evident when Johannes (Hans) Luther was born in 1526. Martin and Katharina's firstborn was named after Luther's father, perhaps, in part, because he had encouraged Martin to get married all along. Hans was the first of six children born in the Luther-von Bora household.

**❹ Elizabeth Luther dies in infancy.**

In 1527, Martin and Katharina's second child, Elizabeth, died at eight months old. Fifteen years later, Martin and Katharina once again experienced the loss of a child, Magdalena, who died at age 13. At Magdalena's funeral, Martin Luther said, "Now I have sent two saints to heaven."

**❺ Martin Luther dies.**

After 20 years of marriage, Martin Luther died on February 18, 1546. In a time when women did not receive inheritances, Martin made Katharina his sole heir. Katharina died in 1552.

*Martin Luther, a former monk, and Katharina von Bora, a former nun, married in June 1525. This marriage is still celebrated in Wittenberg, Germany in June each year.*

# KATHARINA VON BORA'S HERRING BARREL ESCAPE FROM THE CONVENT

*On Easter Eve, 1523, Katharina joined several other nuns in a grand escape. A local merchant from Grimma drove his wagon of goods into the convent and whisked the nuns away. In order to escape undetected (so the story goes) the nuns hid themselves in empty herring barrels.*

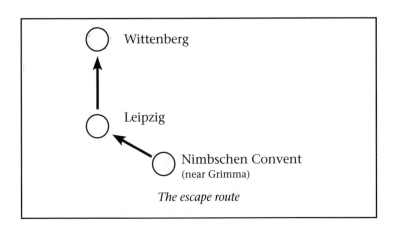

Wittenberg

Leipzig

Nimbschen Convent
(near Grimma)

*The escape route*

*On the Tuesday after Easter, 1523, Katharina
and the other nuns arrived in Wittenberg. The nuns were
well-received and many found husbands there. Katharina was
one of the last to wed. In 1525, she married Wittenberg's
most famous resident: Martin Luther.*

# PORTRAIT OF MARTIN LUTHER

*Martin Luther (1483-1546) is known for spearheading the Reformation. As a monk, he also advocated for the marriage of priests. He himself married a former nun, Katharina von Bora. They were married 20 years at the time of his death. (This illustration of Martin Luther is based on a 1526 portrait by his close friend Lucas Cranach the Elder, who designed woodcut illustrations for Luther's tracts and writings.)*

# PORTRAIT OF
# KATHARINA VON BORA

*Katharina von Bora (1499-1552) escaped from a convent in 1523 and married Martin Luther in 1525. She and Martin had a lively household with six children, as well as boarders and frequent guests. Among her many responsibilities, Katharina or "Katie" grew vegetables, raised cattle and chickens, and brewed beer. (This illustration of Katharina von Bora is based on a 1526 portrait by Lucas Cranach the Elder.)*

# FIVE NOTEWORTHY THINGS MARTIN LUTHER SAID ABOUT MARRIAGE

Martin Luther did not get married until 1525. Nevertheless, Luther went "on record" regarding the subject of marriage as early as 1518. Most noteworthy about these five things is the fact that they were written before Luther himself was married!

*Luther's understanding of marriage as a vocation led him to say that even changing a baby's diapers was part of carrying out God's will.*

**❶** "If God himself does not give the wife or the husband, anything can happen" (*Luther's Works*, 44:8).
Luther was a celibate monk when he wrote these words. Nevertheless, he understood the idea that God should be consulted when contemplating marriage. Years later, Luther reflected upon his brief courtship with the former nun Katharina von Bora: "When I wished to take my Katy I prayed to God earnestly" (*Luther's Works*, 54:26).

**❷** "I advise anyone henceforth being ordained a priest or anything else that he in no way vow to the bishop that he will remain celibate. On the contrary, he should tell the bishop that he has no right whatsoever to require such a vow, and that it is a devilish tyranny to make such a demand" (*Luther's Works*, 44:177).
And with these words, the emptying of the monasteries and convents began!

**❸** " 'Be fruitful and multiply' [Gen. 1:28]. From this passage we may be assured that man and woman should and must come together in order to multiply" (*Luther's Works*, 45:18).
Luther understood marriage as God's First Commandment, and he said having babies was "more necessary than sleeping and waking, eating and drinking, and emptying the bowels and bladder" (*Luther's Works*, 45:18).

**❹** "The greatest good in married life, that which makes all suffering and labor worthwhile, is that God grants offspring" (*Luther's Works*, 45:46).
Luther believed the greatest joy of married life was when children were added to the picture. When Luther did finally marry and have children (six altogether), his view of children was confirmed.

**5** "No one can have real happiness in marriage who does not recognize in firm faith that this estate together with all its works, however insignificant, is pleasing to God and precious in his sight" (*Luther's Works,* 45:42).

Luther understood marriage in terms of vocation. Yes, the duties that come with marriage and family can be difficult, but when these duties are fulfilled with the knowledge that one is doing the will of God, then great is the reward. So, for instance, a father should not complain when he has to change a diaper, but should instead confess to God that he is not worthy to "wash the little babe's diapers, or to be entrusted with the care of the child and its mother" (*Luther's Works*, 45:39).

# FIVE FAITHFUL COUPLES IN THE BIBLE

**❶ Joseph and Mary.**

Mary and Joseph were engaged to be married. When Mary conceived a child through the Holy Spirit, Joseph initially decided not to go through with the marriage. God's angel, however, told Joseph the child Mary carried was of God and would save the people, so Joseph and Mary stayed together and were the parents of the Savior.

**❷ Jacob and Rachel.**

Jacob worked seven years to marry Rachel, but then Rachel's father tricked him into marrying Rachel's sister instead. So Jacob worked seven more years for Rachel. The two then had trouble conceiving children, although eventually they did have children together. They remained faithful to God and each other through it all.

**❸ Ruth and Boaz.**

Ruth was a Moabite widow who had been married to an Israelite man. When her husband died, she stayed with her mother-in-law Naomi, even though Naomi had nothing to offer her. Then Ruth met a man named Boaz, to whom she proved loyal and who in turn proved loyal to her. Their great-grandson was David, king of Israel.

**❹ Abraham and Sarah.**

Yes, Abraham and Sarah were unfaithful, trying to pressure God and trying to keep God's promises by themselves (see "Seven Unfaithful Couples in the Bible"). But they were also faithful to each other and to God. Although they doubted God, they held onto faith through the doubt. Although they doubted whether God would give them children, they stayed with each other and shared the child Isaac, through whom God passed on the blessing promised to them.

**❺ God and sinners.**
Both the Old Testament and the New Testament compare God's relationship with us to a marriage. God is like an ever-faithful spouse. Although we may sin, stray, err, and prove unfaithful to God, God is always faithful—forgiving, accepting us back, and loving us.

*Abraham and Sarah were faithful to each other and to God. Although they doubted God, they held onto faith through the doubt. They stayed with each other and shared the child Isaac, through whom God passed on the blessing promised to them.*

# SEVEN UNFAITHFUL COUPLES IN THE BIBLE

**❶ Ahab and Jezebel.**
The most notorious couple in the Bible may well be Ahab and Jezebel. Ahab, a king of Israel, married the foreigner Jezebel, and the two of them worshiped Baal. They also conspired together to murder and oppress God's faithful people.

**❷ Adam and Eve.**
As soon as God confronted Adam for eating the apple, Adam tried to pass the blame off on Eve: "The woman whom you gave to be with me, she gave me fruit from the tree, and I ate" (Genesis 3:12).

**❸ Abraham and Sarah.**
God had promised the couple children, but they got tired of waiting for God. So Sarah suggested Abraham have a child with her slave girl, Hagar, and Abraham agreed.

**❹ Ananias and Sapphira.**
These two early Christians lied about the price for which they sold some property and withheld gifts owed to God (Acts 5:1–11). They also lied to God and the church.

**❺ Herod and Herodias.**
King Herod Antipas married his brother Philip's wife, Herodias, which was forbidden in God's law (see Mark 6:14–29; Leviticus 18:16). When John the Baptist condemned this sin, Herod imprisoned and then beheaded John.

**❻ David and Bathsheba.**
These two were both married, but to other people. David should have been away at war, like Bathsheba's husband,

Uriah (who was a soldier in David's army). While Uriah was away, David and Bathsheba conceived a child together. To cover up the sin, David arranged to have Uriah killed in battle. Bathsheba later schemed to see that one of her sons, Solomon, became king after David.

**❼ Hosea and Gomer.**
God told Hosea to marry Gomer, even though God promised Hosea that Gomer would be unfaithful. Hosea did marry Gomer, and she was unfaithful. The message in this marriage is that all of us are like unfaithful spouses; we are supposed to be faithful to God, but we all wander away.

*Abraham and Sarah were unfaithful too. God promised them a child, but they got tired of waiting. Sarah suggested that Abraham have a child with her slave girl Hagar, and Abraham agreed.*

# THE FIVE MOST INTERESTING THINGS THE APOSTLE PAUL SAID ABOUT MARRIAGE

**1** "To the unmarried and the widows I say that it is well for them to remain unmarried as I am. But if they are not practicing self-control, they should marry. For It is better to marry than to be aflame with passion" (1 Corinthians 7:8–9).

Paul believed celibacy allowed one to focus on Christ. He also believed attending to marital duties could distract believers from the Christian life, and desire could overwhelm them and keep them from worshiping appropriately. In these cases, marriage provided an acceptable outlet for this passion so the believers could refocus.

**2** "So I would have younger widows marry, bear children, and manage their households, so as to give the adversary no occasion to revile us" (1 Timothy 5:14).

The early Christian community provided for widows when their families cast them out. This freed widows for a special life of prayer as service to the community. However, some widows abused this privilege by taking the community's resources without regard, and even abusing their freedom to enjoy questionable social practices. Paul realized some younger widows could still be wives and mothers, so he encouraged them to rejoin family life so as not to tempt others or corrupt themselves.

❸ "Wife, for all you know, you might save your husband. Husband, for all you know, you might save your wife" (1 Corinthians 7:16).
In the early Christian church, most believers converted as adults regardless of their spouses' beliefs. Paul understood that married life provided an intimacy that promoted conversion. He encouraged believers to not divorce an unbelieving spouse but instead to remain married and exemplify what it meant to follow Christ. In this way the spouse, as well as the children, could come to faith and be saved.

❹ "Each of you, however, should love his wife as himself, and a wife should respect her husband" (Ephesians 5:33).
Many people question Paul's statements on the husband as the head of the wife (for example, see Ephesians 5:22-24) since they sound chauvinistic and oppressive today. However, Paul actually said mutual love and respect belonged in a Christian marriage, and he argued for marital equality. These ideas were revolutionary in the society of the time.

❺ "So then, he who marries his fiancée does well; and he who refrains from marriage will do better" (1 Corinthians 7:38).
Paul believed strongly that Christ would return soon. Believers should not dramatically alter their lives and distract themselves from vigilance for Christ's second coming. Planning too far into the future would only keep one from preparing for Christ. It takes great adjustment to marry, so a believer should instead plan to remain single.

# THE TOP THREE THINGS THE SONG OF SOLOMON SAYS

**❶** "My beloved is mine and I am his; he pastures his flock among the lilies. Until the day breathes and the shadows flee..." (Song of Solomon 2:16–17).

These unabashed words point to a whole night of breathtaking devotion and pleasure, a primary joy of married life.

**❷** "How beautiful you are, my love, how very beautiful!" (Song of Solomon 4:1).

Verses 1-6 are comments about the other's body, made with lavish, erotic detail. Such languorous attention and conversation may well be a tonic for today's "go-go" marriages. Today the words might be, "Slow down," followed by, "Don't be embarrassed."

**❸** "I am my beloved's, and his desire is for me. Come, my beloved, let us go forth into the fields, and lodge in the villages" (Song of Solomon 7:10–11).

Time away with your spouse is always a good idea.

# Dating & Courtship

# TEN RULES FOR THE FIRST DATE

**❶ Remember who you are.**
Stay in touch with your faith and values. Make decisions reflecting who you are, and not who someone else wants you to be.

**❷ Arrive on time.**
Punctuality says something about a person. Arrive within three minutes on either side of the appointed time.

**❸ Be respectful and gracious to your date and those around you.**
Show good manners to those waiting on tables and taking tickets. Avoid flirting with them.

**❹ Bring ample cash.**
Always have enough cash to pay for both of you, even when paying is not an expectation. This may enable you to extricate yourself and your date from an embarrassing situation.

**❺ Eat well.**
Order reasonably priced fare. Eat enough to keep hunger at bay during the balance of the date. Avoid stuffing.

**❻ Dress for the weather.**
You need to feel comfortable in your clothes, so you aren't preoccupied with them. Consider layering.

**❼ Pay attention to your date.**
Listen. Watch for signs of interest or boredom. Make mental notes of important sounding things your date tells you so you can respond at the appropriate time.

**❽ Limit distractions.**

Turn off cell phones and pagers. Avoid looking at your watch.

**❾ Have fun.**

Relax and enjoy yourself. This is a date, not a job interview. Bad dates are often turned around eventually by employing a positive attitude.

**❿ Pray.**

Pray for the Spirit to be present on your date and bless your time together. When unsure of your date's religious predilections, ask permission to pray.

*Flirting with others is not recommended unless you want to avoid a second date.*

# THE TOP 10 ATTRIBUTES TO LOOK FOR IN A SPOUSE

While no single personality trait can predict a compatible marriage, the following list frames the basic things to look for in a spouse. With all attributes, some differences can be the source of a couple's strength rather than a source of difficulty. Statistically, Christians appear to be about as successful at choosing a spouse as other people.

**❶ Similar values.**
Values that concern religious beliefs, life purpose, financial priorities, and children are a foundation on which to build the relationship. Contrary values tend to create discord.

**❷ Physical-energy and physical-space compatibility.**
Consider whether the person's energy level and physical-space needs work with yours. Also, the word *compatibility* can mean a complementary match of opposites, or it can denote a match based on strong similarities.

**❸ Physical and romantic compatibility.**
If the two of you have a similar degree of interest in or need for physical and romantic expression in your relationship, the chance of lifelong compatibility increases.

**❹ Intellectual parity.**
Communicating with someone who has a significantly different intelligence level or educational background can require extra effort.

**❺ Emotional maturity.**
A lifelong relationship of mutual challenge and support often helps each person grow emotionally, but a lifetime spent waiting for someone to grow up could be more frustration than it's worth.

**❻ Sense of humor.**
Sense of humor can provide an excellent measure of a person's personality and an important means to couple survival. If he or she doesn't get your jokes, you could be asking for trouble.

**❼ Respect.**
Look for someone who listens to you without trying to control you. Look also for a healthy sense of self-respect.

**❽ Trustworthiness.**
Seek out someone who is honest and acts with your best interests in mind—not only his or hers—and tries to learn from his or her mistakes.

**❾ Forgiving.**
When you sincerely apologize to your spouse, he or she should try to work through and get beyond the problem rather than hold on to it. Once forgiven, past mistakes should not be raised, especially in conflict situations.

**❿ Kindness.**
An attitude of consistent kindness may be the most critical attribute for a lifelong partnership.

## Please Note

- If you live a long life, you probably will experience major changes that you cannot predict at age 15 or 25 or 35. Accepting this fact in advance can help you weather difficult times.

- Use all of your resources—intuition, emotions, and rational thought—to make the decision about a life partner.

- Family members and trusted friends can offer invaluable advice in this decision-making process and should be consulted.

# HOW TO PROBE FOR YOUR PROSPECTIVE SPOUSE'S TRUE RELIGIOUS VIEWS

**❶** Ask about your prospective spouse's baptism.
Generally, adult baptism indicates a more evangelical believer and infant baptism may point to more mainline views. If your prospective spouse has not been baptized, continue probing.

**❷** Invite your prospective spouse to attend worship with you.
If your invitation is declined, ask where your prospective spouse goes to worship (if at all). If your prospective spouse agrees to join you at worship, watch for evidence of inexperience or ease with the worship service.

**❸** Broach a hot-button subject and gauge the response.
Choose an issue that generally causes disagreements between people of different faiths and denominations. Listen carefully to your prospective spouse's position on this issue.

**❹** Ask friends or family.
Once you gain access to your prospective spouse's inner circle ask key people leading questions about your prospective spouse's weekend activities.

**❺** In case of an emergency, ask directly.
Ask, "So, what do you believe anyway?" Attempt this approach only if all other action fails. Direct questioning can lead to hostility, frustration, and sentimentality.

# THE FIVE BEST SETTINGS FOR POPPING THE QUESTION

Once you decide to propose to your intended spouse, consider three important things: setting, setting, and setting. While your beloved may indeed agree to marry you out of love regardless of your choice of setting you cannot afford to take chances.

**1** During a close, intimate gathering of family and friends.
Choose loved ones who know of and support your union, whose presence puts your loved one at ease. Beware: When this approach backfires the damage can be ruinous. Choose it after great deliberation.

**2** In a public place.
A park, a concert, or a museum can provide a beautiful backdrop for your proposal, as well as supportive bystanders after your beloved says "yes." However, *do not* make this proposal in a very public place, such as onstage at a show, during half-time at a game, or on television, as it places too much pressure on your intended and is cheesy.

**3** In a quiet, one-on-one situation.
If you have any uncertainty at all about the event, choose a private setting. This leaves space for any conversation or emotional outpouring that might occur.

**❹ Immediately following a major event.**
The afterglow of a wedding, trip, or holiday creates
a favorable atmosphere for your proposal. However,
proposing *during* these major events could create
unnecessary tension.

**❺ At a re-creation of a milestone in your relationship.**
Choose an event or location in your mutual history that
would remind your intended of an extremely positive
aspect of your relationship. Make sure you both recall
the same details of the place and event to avoid any
awkwardness.

*The more public the setting, the more you should consider
finding another place to pop the question.*

## Please Note

Regardless of your method, determine the following in advance:

- *Your intended's likely acceptance.* Unless you have both discussed the topic and decided you anticipate lives together, do not propose.

- *The general acceptance of your intended's family.* While you do not have to ask their permission, asking family members for their blessing shows you value their opinion as your future in-laws.

- *A general plan for what you will say.* Your intended will remember what you say at the proposal, so make it good—but don't make it staged or falsely sentimental.

# The Wedding

# THE ANATOMY OF A
# TYPICAL LUTHERAN WEDDING

pianist

soloist

groom

bride

groomsmen

pastor

unity candle &
candelabra

A wedding is merely a blessing of the marriage. The wedding includes promises made in the presence of God as well as witnesses, and it is a worship service. This is the common pattern to Lutheran weddings.

ushers

family

bridesmaids

flower arrangements

**❶ Gathering.**
This could be as simple as you and your guests singing a hymn and the pastor saying a prayer. More often there will be a procession with special music, attendants, and the like.

**❷ Word.**
The Word part of the service involves Scripture readings and a meditation or sermon on those readings. This can be especially meaningful if, in premarital counseling, you select readings that speak to this turning point in your lives and your hope for the future.

**❸ The marriage rite.**
You and your guests may see this as the main thing, because it includes the exchange of vows and rings, but it's just one part of this worship service.

**❹ Meal.**
If your wedding really is a worship service, and if you and most of those attending are regular worshipers, why not include communion? At least consider it.

**❺ Sending.**
The pastor blesses you and your spouse, blesses the assembly, and lets everyone loose to continue the celebration!

# HOW TO PLAN A LUTHERAN WEDDING

Once you and your beloved decide to take the leap together, the planning starts.

**❶ Call the church and get your wedding on the calendar.**
Most churches have guidelines, and many have a wedding coordinator to make your planning easier. (If you don't belong to a congregation, this is the perfect time to find and join one! You'll want to ground your new marriage in the Word and community of God's people.)

**❷ Begin premarital counseling or classes.**
Your church probably offers this. The point is to focus on the marriage, not just the wedding. It's easier to think "marriage" if you complete this step six months before your wedding.

**❸ Make a wedding budget and stick to it.**
Talk with your beloved (and your parents) about who will pay for what. Don't spend a great deal. Avoid using credit where possible.

**❹ Plan for a wedding ceremony that is a worship service.**
Jesus Christ, and our faith in him, is the focus.

- Choose at least one hymn—this invites everyone to participate in your wedding, not just witness it.

- Select songs of faith; save your favorite love song for the reception.

- Give careful thought to the Bible readings you select. Visit with your pastor about this.

- Use competent, experienced musicians. Pay them well.

- If the service includes communion, it should by no means be offered only to the bridal party; invite all Christians.

## Please Note

- Things will not always work out the way you pictured them. You will need to compromise on dates, the guest list, facilities, and many other arrangements. Remain flexible. Keep your sense of humor.

*Instruct videographers and photographers to position themselves unobtrusively, so as to avoid damaging the sanctity of the event.*

# HOW TO SELECT YOUR MAID OF HONOR OR BEST MAN

When selecting a maid of honor or best man, it is important he or she meet several criteria.

**❶ Dependability.**
He or she must be willing and able to show up for all the activities related to the position.

*Do not compromise on the criteria when choosing a best man or maid of honor. Dependability and a calming presence are essential.*

**❷ Supportiveness.**
He or she must be able to care for you during times of chaos, excitement, doubt, and tantrums.

**❸ A calming presence.**
Avoid selecting someone who will grate on your nerves when either of you are under pressure.

**❹ Willingness to work.**
A maid of honor or best man needs to be willing to run around at the last minute and during the planning stages to attend to your needs.

**❺ Financial ability to meet your expectations.**
A maid of honor and best man will be responsible for paying for outfits, parties, travel, and gifts, at the minimum. Do not ask someone living on macaroni and cheese to strain him or herself financially.

## Please Note

• Family and friends will have opinions and expectations about whom you should choose. Let the criteria be your guide instead.

# HOW TO MAKE MUTUALLY SATISFACTORY DECISIONS ABOUT THE WEDDING

While weddings are a source of great joy, they are also a source of high stress. When stress and anxiety escalate, conflict usually follows. Anticipate the issues that will surface as you plan your wedding so you can decide how you will handle them in advance.

❶ Finances.

Do research so you have an idea how much you plan to spend. Talk to your parents and share your cost research. Decide how much each party can contribute. Scale back your plans if necessary.

❷ Date and place.

Seek input from your families as you plan a date. Avoid dates that conflict with other special family events, like graduations. Make sure both the pastor and the church are available on the day of the wedding. Do this before you sign with a reception hall or engrave your invitations.

❸ Traditions and expectations.

Talk to parents about their hopes for the day. Both bride and groom should talk about how they envision the day unfolding. If there are differences in expectations, negotiate. This is a skill you will need during marriage, too.

**4** Faith traditions.
Talk about your expectations for the wedding ceremony itself. This is especially important if the bride and groom come from different faith backgrounds. Include your pastor(s) in this conversation. Ask what rules the church has regarding wedding ceremonies. Respect them.

**5** The bridal party.
Who's in and who's not can be a touchy subject. Some friends and family may assume you'll ask them to be in the bridal party. You might not. Consider other ways to include close friends and family members who aren't in the bridal party.

**6** Invitations.
Based on expenses, decide how many people you can invite. The bride and groom should each make a list of close friends and family. Ask your parents who they would like to include on the list.

**7** Seating arrangements.
Use care in organizing seating arrangements for the reception. As you plan, consider the personalities of people, family estrangements, and past conflicts. The day will be more fun if a brawl doesn't break out.

**8** Gift registry.
Share gift registry information with family and friends. This will help prevent gift duplication and the dilemma of deciding whose toaster to keep and whose to return when you receive two.

## Please Note

- Don't be afraid when conflict does occur. It's how you deal with it that counts.

- It is advisable for the parents of both bride and groom to meet and develop a relationship before the wedding planning begins.

- Emotions and stress will increase as your wedding day approaches. Make an extra effort to keep your communications healthy. Consider jogging or some other cardiovascular workout to deal with pre-wedding stress.

*Tell your friends and family about your gift registry to prevent the dilemma caused by duplicate gifts.*

# THE FIVE MOST OVERUSED WEDDING BIBLE READINGS

**1** 1 Corinthians 13: The "Love Chapter."
This is an ode to perfect, Christ-like love. Such love is not a quality; it's a gift (12:31). See how much you need it by substituting your name wherever the word *love* appears in verses 4–7.

**2** 1 John 4:7–8: "Beloved, let us love one another, because love is from God... for God is love."
Love, in all its forms, is from God. The love you and your beloved share is God's gift. Don't quit with verse 8; add 9 and 10 so everyone at your wedding will hear that God loves and redeems them in Jesus Christ.

**3** Ruth 1:16–17: "Where you go, I will go... your people shall be my people, and your God my God."
The ancient story tells how Ruth, a young widow, meets and marries a good man. The popular quote is not what Ruth says to this man, however; it is her expression of loyalty to her mother-in-law.

**4** Ecclesiastes 4:9–12: "Two are better than one.... A threefold cord is not quickly broken."
Practical advice (though not particularly profound or spiritual) for keeping warm and using the "buddy system."

**5** Mark 10:7–9: "For this reason a man shall leave his father and mother and be joined to his wife, and the two shall become one flesh."
In Mark, Jesus quotes Genesis 2:24 while sparring with Pharisees about divorce. You might choose the Genesis passage (2:18–24) instead.

# FIVE FRESH WEDDING BIBLE READINGS

❶ Matthew 18:19–20: "Again, truly I tell you, if two of you agree on earth about anything you ask, it will be done for you by my Father in heaven. For where two or three are gathered in my name, I am there among them."
In the Gospels, words of love involve asking and serving.

❷ Colossians 3:12–15: "As God's chosen ones, holy and beloved, clothe yourselves with compassion, kindness, humility, meekness, and patience. Bear with one another and, if anyone has a complaint against another, forgive each other; just as the Lord has forgiven you, so you also must forgive. Above all, clothe yourselves with love, which binds everything together in perfect harmony. And let the peace of Christ rule in your hearts, to which indeed you were called in the one body. And be thankful."
Paul speaks of love in broad terms, while calling for specific attributes in relationships. (See also Philippians 4:4–9.)

❸ Isaiah 55:10–12: "For as the rain and the snow come down from heaven, and do not return there until they have watered the earth, making it bring forth and sprout, giving seed to the sower and bread to the eater, so shall my word be that goes out from my mouth; it shall not return to me empty, but it shall accomplish that which I purpose, and succeed in the thing for which I sent it. For you shall go out in joy, and be led back in peace; the mountains and the hills before you shall burst into song, and all the trees of the field shall clap their hands."

Several Old Testament prophets offer words of hope and fulfillment. Passages such as this one and Jeremiah 31:2–5 might be of particular interest to those who are marrying for the second time.

**4** Song of Solomon 2:3–4: "As an apple tree among the trees of the wood, so is my beloved among young men. With great delight I sat in his shadow, and his fruit was sweet to my taste. He brought me to the banqueting house, and his intention toward me was love."

Coming from a rich tradition of sacred wedding songs from the Near East, passages from this poem speak of passionate love using descriptive words from God's created natural world.

**5** Psalm 33:20–22: "Our soul waits for the Lord; he is our help and shield. Our heart is glad in him, because we trust in his holy name. Let your steadfast love, O Lord, be upon us, even as we hope in you."

The songs and poetry from Psalms speak of joy and give praise to God. God can be praised for the gracious gift of a life partner.

# THE FIVE MOST OVERUSED WEDDING SONGS

The music used during the wedding ceremony can contribute greatly to an appropriate, worshipful atmosphere. Choosing selections that are enormously popular and stereotypical, however, may distract from the spirit of the event.

**❶** "Wedding March," by Richard Wagner.
Better known as "Here Comes the Bride."

**❷** "Canon," by Johann Pachelbel.
Certain to make the ceremony feel like a TV commercial for wine.

**❸** "Trumpet Voluntary (The Prince of Denmark's March)," by Jeremiah Clarke.
Became a "hit" following its use in the wedding of Prince Charles and Princess Diana.

**❹** "The Wedding Song (There Is Love)," by Noel Paul Stookey.
This 1970s-era folk song is often the default selection if the wedding soloist is a guitarist.

**❺** "I Will Be Here," by Steven Curtis Chapman.
Frequently used by couples who are fans of contemporary Christian music.

## Please Note

- If you absolutely must use worn-out or clichéd wedding music, be sure your instrumentalist or soloist is an excellent musician. Bad music played well is better than bad music played badly.

# FIVE FRESH WEDDING SONGS

**❶** Consider an old standard not usually sung at weddings.
One hymn that works well is "Joyful, Joyful, We Adore Thee" because the tune is from Beethoven's Ninth Symphony.

**❷** Sing a new song.
"This Is a Day, LORD, Gladly Awaited" is a new song to the tune of the old Gaelic folksong "Morning Has Broken," which Cat Stevens made popular before he changed his name.

**❸** There's more than one "Trumpet Tune."
If you're going for loud, rousing processional music—the better to get people to stop chatting and stand up—there are lots of great trumpet tunes.

**❹** 1 Corinthians 13 can be musical.
"Although I Speak with Angel's Tongue" and "The Gift of Love" are reliable solo settings of this famous passage.

**❺** Commission a new song.
For the price of a couple of tuxedo rentals you can probably get something really fresh.

# HOW TO LIGHT THE UNITY CANDLE WITHOUT SETTING THE BRIDE'S HAIR ON FIRE

**1** Use candles that are not too high, too heavy, or too thick.
Standard-size candlesticks about one inch in diameter will be easier to maneuver and will give off shorter flames. Note: Always trim candlewicks and test-light them in advance.

**2** Ask the bride to sweep back her veil (if any) and hair prior to the lighting.

**3** Encourage the bride to point the lighter candle away from her veil.
Grasp the candle at arm's length, tilting it away from the body with elbow slightly bent.

**4** Keep the unity candle ceremony brief. Avoid lengthy musical accompaniment.
The longer the bride (and groom) stand holding dripping candles, the more likely a mishap.

## Please Note

• Certain hairsprays and gels are flammable and thus increase the chances of hair catching flame.

• No precautions will do much good if the bride trips on her train! Make sure the train is arranged neatly behind her, and avoid the combination of very high heels and steep steps.

*The bride and groom should grasp their candles gently but firmly. Do not force the candle out if it doesn't come easily. Slowly twist your candle until it loosens.*

❶

*Lift your candles straight up to a position slightly above the unity candle.*

❷

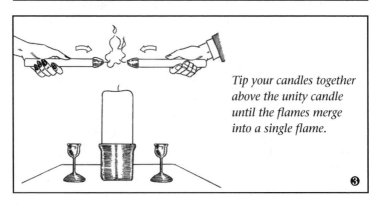

*Tip your candles together above the unity candle until the flames merge into a single flame.*

❸

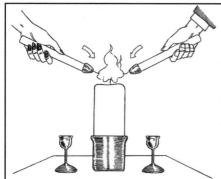

Lower your candles together, keeping the flames joined, and touch the flame to the unlit wick of the unity candle.

❹

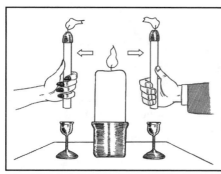

Return your candles to the upright position above their holders. Do not extinguish your flame.

❺

Gently place your candle back into its holder. This completes the lighting of the unity candle. You may need to wait several awkward minutes for your music selection to end. This is normal. Gaze fondly into your new spouse's eyes.

❻

# FIVE COMMON WEDDING CEREMONY EMERGENCIES AND HOW TO HANDLE THEM

While stories of runaway brides and cold-footed grooms are legend, real wedding emergencies often fall along the lines of everyday headaches run amok.

**❶ A member of the wedding party is late.**
Act naturally; allow stragglers to get seated without causing a scene. Make sure the musicians are prepared to pad any extra time in this event.

**❷ The bride or groom cracks under the pressure.**
Small setbacks and surprises can derail a normally even-keeled person. The maid of honor or best man must step in to restore calm and decorum with reassuring eye contact, an assured smile, and a gentle touch.

**❸ "The rings. Where are the rings?"**
Simply carry on. The rings are a symbol of this union between man, woman, and God—not the actual mystery itself.

**❹ A groomsman or bridesmaid faints.**
Consider designating a first responder to attend the wedding to assist in such cases. After the responder seats the fainted person safely and their welfare is safeguarded, continue the service as planned. Allow the light-headed person to remain seated; send a runner for a glass of water.

**❺ A guest disrupts the ceremony.**
If someone is determined to make a scene, there's likely little you can do to stop them, but a quick response will help mitigate the damage. Signal the ushers and/or groomsmen to escort the person from the sanctuary—using force only if necessary. Carry on once the dust has settled.

*Any of these factors can induce fainting: knees locked in place, insufficient nutrition, excessive drinking, lack of sleep, and uncomfortable shoes. Take preventive measures and designate a first-aid responder in advance.*

# The First Year

# HOW TO TRAIN YOUR SPOUSE

Accept reality: God made your spouse with a will, a mind, and a life of his or her own. If you don't like this, take it up with God. If you attempt to train your spouse to obey you all the time, expect high levels of frustration, anxiety, and retaliation. But, if you insist on trying...

**❶ Avoid unrealistic expectations of your spouse.**
Your spouse may be barely human, but is still only human.

**❷ Avoid losing your temper.**
Anger does not contribute to healthy change.

**❸ DO NOT attempt to make changes in areas even training experts avoid.**
Some training events fail before they start, such as anything related to the car or the bathroom. Realize quickly that significant behavioral change cannot occur in these areas, and instead pick worthwhile training opportunities.

**❹ Consider using a pet name.**
Develop a list of pet names that you can interchange without suspicion, such as "sweetie," "pumpkin pie," and "muffin." (If you use the same pet name every time you want something, your spouse will immediately have his or her guard up.) The more nauseating the name, the more surprising and endearing it will be to your spouse.

**❺ Establish a pattern.**
If you have a particular pet peeve or request, state it early and often. By creating a consistent pattern for your spouse to follow, your spouse will learn quickly what behaviors you desire.

**⑥ Utilize available positive stimuli.**
The human animal responds strongly to food. Try preparing a favorite meal or bringing home a special treat. While the spouse enjoys the food, propose and reinforce training points.

*If all else fails, simply accept your spouse as a gift from God.*

**❼** Articulate your requests in a way that renders them undeniable.

Say, "You could do this, couldn't you?" or "It would really mean so much to me if you took care of this." Questions or statements like these build your spouse's confidence and encourage him or her to demonstrate ability in these areas in the future.

**❽** Display strong emotion.

By placing emotional weight on the event, you invest more in the action. Be sure to choose the emotion carefully, however. Anger could frustrate and discourage the spouse, while vulnerability can inspire.

## Please Note

- Training takes great time and effort for you and for your spouse. Make sure you consistently reward good behavior and do not dwell on bad behavior. Together, you can both create an optimal environment of mutually beneficial interaction.

- If all else fails, accept your spouse as a gift from God and consider that you may be the one who needs to change.

- If your spouse is physically abusive, abuses drugs, or engages in other criminal or dangerous behavior, seek professional help immediately.

# HOW TO MERGE
# HOUSEHOLD POSSESSIONS

Idyllic unity meets stark reality when two people try to merge their stuff. "His" desk becomes "our" desk, and he can count on a drawer or two less. "Her Volkswagen" is now "our bug." And that's just the beginning, so it's best to start with clear communication.

**❶ Surrender to the process of becoming a single unit.**
This is generally fun. Sure, there will be stressful times. There will be give and take, as with everything in life. But you'll grow as a person as you each grow as spouses.

**❷ Have fun with recognizing and understanding your spouse's tastes and opinions.**
Learning to appreciate your spouse may start with some of the stuff he or she brings into the household.

**❸ Avoid employing a "win/lose" attitude.**
No one should keep score about who gets "their" way. Expect much negotiation and much giving-in on both accounts.

**❹ You don't need two...whatevers.**
You really don't. And don't bother saving one for when the other breaks, because you won't be able to find it anyway.

**❺ Who's got the best taste?**
This is impossible to figure out. Negotiate on the "public" areas of the home. Find less noticeable areas for his (tacky) poker painting or her (frilly) doll collection.

## Please Note

- Stuff is just stuff. It's not important enough to jeopardize your relationship.

- Negotiate about the stuff that is most important to you. Express yourself with passion, but don't hold too tightly. Give room for discussion.

- Consider donating some of your stuff to a local charity.

- If stuff doesn't fit your living space, dump it. You really won't ever miss the stuff stored away in boxes.

*When you merge household possessions, there will be some give and take, as with everything in life. Learning to appreciate your spouse may start with tolerating some of his or her stuff (junk).*

# HOW TO MERGE
# HOUSEHOLD FINANCES

Finances can be troublesome in any marriage. Solutions revolve around clear communication, realistic expectations, and a certain amount of discipline.

**1** **Pray regularly about where your money goes.**
Be completely honest about spending. This is the starting point for conversations with your spouse about finances too.

**2** **Consider using a single, shared checkbook.**
Holding finances together helps with decision-making, although it may not always seem so. This also helps develop communication habits that will be useful for a lifetime.

**3** **Develop a habit of paying by cash. Avoid debt whenever possible.**
If you don't use actual currency, using debit cards and credit cards that you pay off every month amount to the same thing. Debt hampers financial freedom and tends to breed more debt.

**4** **Commit together to budgeted charitable giving and strict monthly savings.**
These essential stewardship areas can build a sense of community that in turn creates a sense of shared mission.

**5** **Give each person an allowance.**
No matter how little you earn, set aside a small portion for fun, occasional treats. This reduces frustration with daily thrift.

**❻ Expect the process of merging finances to take time.** Building realistic expectations about money takes a lifetime of work in the best of cases, so you can expect that building common and realistic expectations as a couple will also take time. Avoid bailing out on account of short-term difficulties.

*Set an intermediate savings goal, like a weekend away, and work toward it together.*

**❼ Salt your finances with plenty of conversation.**
Talk about current spending and saving habits and
patterns. Regular discussions about spending and saving
help clear the air and can lead to a deeper relationship.
Tell stories about how money was spent in your
household of origin, to help understand each other's
habits and values.

**❽ Establish intermediate goals to understand the
power of saving together.**
Saving for a weekend away is a tangible short-term goal
that can invigorate both partners. Discuss larger goals,
such as home ownership and financial ministry through
your congregation. Working toward goals helps put your
present spending patterns in the right light.

# HOW TO SHARE A CAR

**❶ Start with one, stay with one.**
Engaged or newly married couples should consider
committing to owning a single vehicle voluntarily. You
haven't yet become accustomed to and dependent on the
convenience of using multiple cars.

**❷ Choose to live near your workplace(s).**
Look for a home in an area conveniently located near
your job(s). You'll be much less likely to need two cars if
you're in close proximity to work.

**❸ Choose to work near your home.**
If you have established a home and are unwilling or
unable to move closer to work, consider finding a new
job with a shorter commute.

**❹ Avail yourselves of alternative transportation
sources.**
Subways, trains, buses, carpools, bicycles, and your own
feet are great modes of travel when you need to trek to
work, go shopping, or get to church.

**❺ Calculate your savings.**
Estimate the amount of money per month you would be
spending on payments, maintenance, insurance, and fuel
if you owned an additional car. Multiply that amount by 12
to see how much money you're saving each year. Estimate
how much you'll save in a decade. Grin accordingly.

**6** Plan ahead for minimal car usage.
Conduct occasional family schedule meetings and compare calendars with your spouse. Arrange any pickups and drop-offs and decide who needs to use the car for specific events or trips.

**7** Respect your spouse's need for time alone with the car.
It is a sacrifice and an inconvenience to share a car, which is a symbol of individual freedom. Be sensitive to your spouse's need for personal space, cleanliness, and scheduling. Ask politely about the vehicle's availability and be flexible regarding your own travel plans.

*Sharing a car can lead to more time together.*

## Please Note

- Be prepared to get a reputation among friends and colleagues as "that person who always needs a ride." Also consider making it a habit to always leave a dollar or three behind in the car seat.

- You may find that one of the unintended positive outcomes of sharing a car is many more hours of quality time with your spouse.

# HOW TO MAINTAIN YOUR OWN FRIENDSHIPS

When two people marry, they form a new family unit, yet each is still an individual. It is important to have friends outside of your marriage to maintain your own identity.

**❶ Cultivate your own interests and hobbies.**
This will give you the opportunity to meet new friends and develop relationships outside your marriage.

**❷ Do lunch.**
Whether you work at home or at an office, schedule regular lunch dates with friends as a means of keeping a healthy perspective. Choose friends with wide-ranging backgrounds and interests.

**❸ Make a regular effort to keep in touch.**
Keep your friends updated on what's happening in your life. Phone or e-mail one another on a regular basis. Consider scheduling correspondence on a monthly rotating basis.

**❹ Introduce your friends to your spouse. Consider arranging for a regular gathering of your friends in your home.**
Your spouse will need to feel comfortable with your friendships. This is especially important if you have a friend of the opposite sex.

**❺ Agree on appropriate boundaries.**
If a friend regularly interrupts your dinnertime with phone calls, this could cause problems. Make sure your friends respect your need for personal space. Program your answering machine to take dinnertime calls.

**6** Maintain confidences with your spouse and your friends.

Avoid telling casual friends deeply intimate information about your spouse or your marriage. To do so can be a breach of trust and cause damaging rifts in the event of a leak.

## Please Note

- Friendships you have enjoyed for many years may be easier to maintain because both parties in these relationships have already invested considerable time. New friendships may require additional effort, at first.

- Friendships are good for your health. People who interact regularly with friends tend to have stronger immune systems.

*Maintaining friendships, while very important, should not impinge unduly upon important aspects of your marriage.*

# THE FIVE MOST IMPORTANT THINGS TO REMEMBER WHEN CHOOSING YOUR FIRST HOME

**❶ Your need for "sacred space."**

Can the property accommodate a special, set-aside place for prayer? Creating art? Reading? Quiet time? This can be accomplished even in a one-bedroom apartment, for example, by converting an enclosed porch or walk-in closet into a reading room. Without dedicated sacred space, any living quarters will turn claustrophobic.

**❷ Considerate neighbors.**

Get acquainted with your neighbors and assess their trustworthiness. Knowing which are good neighbors is paramount, especially when you get locked out or need someone to watch your place while on vacation.

**❸ Soundness of structures and fixtures.**

Bring a checklist for the following items: condition of kitchen appliances, roofing, heating, air conditioning, flooding history, structural soundness of deck (especially on upper floors), windows, and sealing around doors. Especially when buying, hire a house inspector to walk through and identify potentially costly repairs.

**❹ Weigh the "investment" required to bring the property up to your standards.**

Even if your find is structurally sound, it may not suit your tastes in color scheme, floor plan, or bathroom tiling. If that's the case, do you stand ready to commit finances and time to fix it up?

**❺ Is it welcoming?**

As a Christian household, you'll want to consider whether you'll feel comfortable hosting Bible studies, parties, prayer gatherings, and interventions. Also important: Will this place seem inviting to you and your family after long days at work and school?

*Find a home surrounded by good neighbors. You'll be glad you did.*

## Please Note

- Never commit to a property beyond your current financial means! Falling behind on rent or mortgage not only damages your credit rating, it could leave you homeless.

- Eccentric landlords exist. Ask about any unusual conditions that may accompany a rental property (for example, reasons for not refunding security deposits) and if possible, talk to other tenants.

# HOW TO DECORATE A LUTHERAN HOME

Married couples can utilize artistic and religious items to make their home a distinctly Lutheran environment.

**❶ A simple cross.**
A cross or crucifix is a welcome addition to the wall of any Christian home.

**❷ "Grace," a photograph by Eric Enstrom.**
Taken in 1918, this famous photograph of an elderly man praying over a loaf of bread is found in many Christian homes in America, and around the world as well.

**❸ Prayer artwork and needlework.**
Many Lutheran homes exhibit the words of prayers done in calligraphy or cross-stitching. Various texts are represented, including the Lord's Prayer, table grace, or other traditional prayers. Often these are written in the language of the family's ancestral homeland.

**❹ Musical instruments.**
Lutherans can uphold the long tradition of singing by keeping musical instruments in their homes. In addition to providing a method of making music, the instruments themselves are often beautiful works of art.

**❺ A home altar.**
Some Lutherans designate a special place in the home where they can focus during personal devotions. This space could include a Bible, candles, and small colored paraments or hangings that change according to the seasons of the church calendar.

# Please Note

- Although nailing documents to a door is an integral part of Lutheran tradition, remember that modern doors made of metal or particle board are not built to withstand the blows of a hammer. Hang your artwork on sturdy walls using nails and hooks instead.

*Hanging in many Lutheran homes is the painting, "Grace," which captures much about the Lutheran perspective regarding God's gracious abundance.*

# HOW TO CHOOSE A CHURCH HOME TOGETHER

Whether you've never been members of a congregation, have decided to seek out a different congregation to join, or have moved to a new town, finding a church community is an important part of a Christian couple's life together.

**❶ Pray together.**
Ask the Holy Spirit to guide you on your search for a church home.

**❷ Get advice from friends and relatives in the area.**
Trusted friends and family members can suggest congregations to visit. Ask to accompany them to their own place of worship.

**❸ Use the Internet.**
Perform an online search for churches in your area. View the results and access available congregation Web sites. Many congregations have a home page featuring worship service schedules, contact information, directions, staff directories, and ministry opportunities.

**❹ Browse the local Yellow Pages or phone directory.**
Look up "churches" in the business listings of your phone book. Congregations often feature small ads and worship service schedules in addition to their addresses and phone numbers.

**❺ Listen for bells and singing.**
Many churches ring loud bells hourly and at the beginning of worship services. The sound of a large group singing is also a good sign that a church may be nearby.

**❻** Look for steeples—and more.

Church buildings can often be seen from a distance due to large bell towers and tall spires topped by crosses. However, many excellent churches meet in ordinary office-buildings, warehouses and even public school buildings. Remain alert to clumps of joyful people on Sunday mornings and Saturday evenings.

*Use the Internet or browse your local Yellow Pages as you begin your search for a church home together.*

**7** Research the beliefs and practices of denominations and congregations.
Note the values and theological positions of the churches you visit. Make sure you share (or tolerate) those views before committing to join a congregation.

**8** Visit a variety of churches.
Experience congregations that are large and small, formal and informal, new and established.

**9** Consider the children.
If you already have children, or anticipate growing your family some time in the future, find out what children's and youth ministries are offered by the congregation.

**10** Compromise.
Spouses may differ about what to expect from their church-going experience. Work together and prepare to sacrifice some of your personal preferences in order to find a congregation you both can agree on.

**11** Determine if you are welcomed.
Evaluate the congregation's response to your presence. Did the pastor greet you? Did other worshipers notice you? Did you meet anyone personally? Did anyone ask for your name?

## Please Note

- Begin your search close to where you live. If you join a church within walking distance or a short drive from your home, you'll be more likely to attend during busy times or in bad weather. In addition, you may meet more people from your neighborhood, and you'll save on travel time and fuel expenses.

- When a person who has been an active member of a congregation gets married, it may be intimidating for their new spouse to join the church. The veteran parishioner should take special care to ensure the spouse is welcomed and informed.

- No church home is perfect.

# HOW TO ESTABLISH A ROUTINE OF DAILY DEVOTIONS

Daily nourishment of the entire being allows people to remain healthy. A routine of daily devotions can produce energy in you and your spouse and stimulate your minds, hearts, and spirits in such a way that you are deeply nourished.

❶ Schedule a daily encounter with God's written Word and time for reflection and integration of that Word into your daily lives. Engage in mutual conversation about the meaning of the Scripture.

❷ Commit to a time for cooperative communication with God through prayer.
Name those who are dear to you both, those who are in need, and those who suffer; lift up your own needs before God; and give thanks for blessings of all kinds.

❸ Allow for experiences that are less structured and more spontaneous. These may include:
- Praying "on the run," in the car, at soccer games, in restaurants, and so on.
- Exploring various devotional materials with different styles from a variety of writers. A wide variety will enrich your devotional life and deepen your shared spiritual vocabulary.
- Writing your own devotions in a diary format or through journaling.
- Singing your prayers out loud or using the poetry of hymns as a devotional resource.

## Please Note

- There is no right or wrong way to do this. You and your spouse might observe some aspects of daily devotions together and others separately. Whatever you do, talk about what you're experiencing and learning.

- Don't beat yourself up if your routine loses its consistency along the way. You and your spouse can help each other by holding each other accountable for keeping the routines in place.

# HOW TO KEEP CHRIST AT THE CENTER OF A MARRIAGE

A Christ-centered marriage is no accident. It takes work. While God supplies marriages with great attention and care, the couple, if they wish their marriage to bear the marks of Christ, must want it to be so and must be willing to make sacrifices for a greater joy. A Christ-centered marriage is like a Christ-centered life.

❶ **Make every effort to avoid sexual sin even before getting married.**
Avoid exposing your future marriage to prior injury. Stay focused. Reject in-the-moment temptations in favor of achieving your goal of a lifelong, monogamous, Christ-centered marriage.

❷ **When possible, seek a partner who already knows Jesus as his or her Lord and Savior.**
Insofar as you are able to control with whom you fall in love, attempt to select persons of a like mind with regard to Christ. If either or both of you come to faith later on, post-wedding, a Christ-centered marriage is still possible and may even yield unique fruits of joy.

❸ **Ask God early on to give both of you the same heart.**
In prayer together, ask God to give you common desires and common direction. Most crucially, ask God to give both of you desires that fit where God wants you to go. This will help get things off on the right foot.

**④** Pray together regularly.

Even a lifetime of praying together does not inoculate against trouble, but it does give two people opportunity for discussion, mediation, and hope when things get difficult—as they surely will. Note: Maintaining this habit can become extremely difficult as time progresses; endeavor to persevere. With time, it will pay off.

**⑤** Try always to keep a clean slate with the other person. Make it a part of your daily ritual together.

Attempt to build a relationship in which you are unafraid to tell each other your innermost thoughts. Rather than your spouse questioning your humanity, you may find that he or she actually grows closer to you because you seek his or her help with a flaw and you are serious about needing help.

**⑥** Don't let the sun go down on your anger. Resolve to settle differences before they accumulate and become an unmanageable burden.

This biblical mandate makes good sense. It is best not to let problems pile up. Consider using your daily prayer or devotional times as opportunities to confess and be done with wrongdoing.

**⑦** Attend church together and reflect on your encounter with Christ's presence.

Provide yourselves time to be in awe of God in each other's company. Share Bible verses at unexpected times of the day. Go to the mountains and experience God's majesty. Give yourselves time to rest and don't always be quick to leave to do other tasks.

**8** Make laughter a priority.

No marriage can survive without humor, and a Christ-centered marriage is especially dependent on it. As your commitment to God can place you at odds with the culture around you, a healthy sense of humor is crucial. Laugh at yourself before you allow yourself to laugh at your spouse.

## Please Note

- Keeping Christ at the center of a marriage means bringing changes and troubles to Christ and to each other as the years progress.

- Choosing to place Christ at the center of your marriage is a willful act of defiance. More the norm are marriages that lack a center, or that center on the wrong things.

# HOW TO NEGOTIATE WHERE YOU GO FOR THE HOLIDAYS

**❶ Pick one family per holiday.**

Even if your families live close to one another, focus on dealing with one side at a time. Flip a coin to see whose family is first.

*Negotiate and compromise to prevent holidays from coming between you.*

**❷** Balance major and minor holidays.
For example, spend the Christmas holiday with one side but Thanksgiving and New Year's Eve with another. Factor into your calculations how much weight each family places on particular holidays.

**❸** Consider highly-valued traditions, especially time-specific ones.
Some families have especially strong holiday-related traditions, which might become stronger as family members grow older. Make an effort to respect these strong traditions while promoting the development of new ones.

**❹** Keep track. Consider negotiating when genuine issues arise that conflict with the schedule.
Did you spend last Easter with your in-laws? Then you can fairly request this Easter with your family. Make sure to document your holiday visits to avoid confrontation with your spouse.

**❺** Consider length of separation from family.
If for some reason you will not see one side of the family for a length of time, use a holiday to break up the separation. Consider this even if it means interrupting a previous holiday visit pattern.

# HOW TO PREVENT IN-LAW ENCROACHMENT

Several areas of possible encroachment may threaten: finances, cleaning, cooking, children, employment, personal habits, faith practices, and holidays. Use these guidelines to open a discussion with your spouse prior to your wedding. Engage in follow-up discussions throughout your marriage.

❶ **Agree on boundaries.**
Decide together what areas are off limits to discussion with in-laws. If an in-law brings up something off limits, politely let the person know the topic is not open to discussion. You might say, "I appreciate your concern, but we want to decide together how to choose your retirement home."

❷ **Set clear expectations.**
Knowing and articulating these expectations as a couple is very helpful when an encroaching in-law does not agree with a decision.

❸ **Back each other up. Always present a united front to all in-laws.**
In cases where you are not completely satisfied with a decision but have agreed to it, you must stand by it with your full endorsement. Use the word "we" in your responses to in-laws.

❹ **Allow for acceptable areas of encroachment.**
Because families love one another, in-laws often experience a need to give advice as an expression of love. Seeking and accepting advice in certain areas can forge

indestructible bonds and further define your relationship with your in-laws.

❺ **Communicate the expectations and boundaries early and often.**
Consider the personalities of all parties when deciding who will broach a given tender subject with in-laws. A new daughter-in-law or son-in-law must possess guts and tact to carry this out effectively.

## Please Note

•   It is permissible to listen to advice from in-laws. It is not permissible to act on the advice without conversation with and support from your spouse.

*Reduce in-law encroachment by setting firm boundaries and sticking to them.*

# HOW TO PREPARE FOR AN IN-LAW VISIT

**❶ Clean your home thoroughly.**
While some in-laws may indeed care whether you dusted behind the pictures on the wall, typically they do not. Cleaning simply gives you the illusion of control over the situation.

*Cleaning before an in-law visit may not be necessary, but it does give you a temporary sense of control.*

**❷ Stock up on material assistance.**
Keep plenty of the in-laws' favorite beverages, treats, and reading materials readily available for their comfort and enjoyment. Ask your spouse not only for good options but also which things to avoid.

**❸ Set the stage.**
Any housewares, articles of clothing, or jewelry items the in-laws have given you should be prominently and tastefully displayed. Try to achieve this naturally. Forced or falsely displayed items are easily detected.

**❹ Plan events, but be flexible according to the in-laws' needs and desires.**
Create occasions for interacting with one another that do not force conversation. Consider a concert or cultural event, as well as social time involving sympathetic friends and family members.

**❺ Give them an honorable out.**
Provide an event your in-laws will enjoy without you. Promote this special occasion as a treat planned as a gift for them. Do not under any circumstances reveal that it simply gives you some time without them to regroup.

# HOW TO RESPOND TO AN IN-LAW'S NOSY QUESTION

Assume, for example, that your in-law has just said, "I want a grandchild; when are you and my child planning on having a baby?"

**❶ The statue.**
A non-aggressive strategy is to pretend that you are a statue and act as if you did not hear the question. Instead, say something like this in a bright tone: "I have been meaning to ask you some advice ... do you think that we should repaint the bedroom ourselves or does that sort of project put too much stress on a couple's relationship?"

**❷ The family system.**
A moderately aggressive strategy is to confuse your in-law with his or her own family system. Look puzzled for a moment and say, "Well, that is really something that you would have to ask your child. Because of his or her experience growing up, your child is reluctant to start a family right now."

❸ The feigned disbelief.
A more aggressive strategy is to clean out your ear with your pinky, and exclaim, "I am sorry, but I must not have heard you correctly, because I thought that you just asked when we were planning on starting a family!"

❹ "Right back at you."
The most aggressive strategy is to place the entire subject back in your in-law's lap. Turn, look your in-law straight in the eye, and say, "If you want a baby, you can look into adoption. There are many children who would benefit greatly from growing up in a home such as yours."

The "statue" strategy can be an effective first-response method of deflecting the nosy in-law.

# SEVEN COMMON MOMENTS IN WHICH YOU SHOULD THINK BEFORE YOU SPEAK

If You Are a Male...

**1** When your wife leaves the driver's seat in the forward position and you crack your kneecap.

**2** When your wife spends more money than budgeted to buy new fancy drawer liners.

**3** When your wife announces she has promised her mother that you will spend your anniversary with your in-laws.

**4** When your wife asks you if her new jeans make her look fat.

**5** When you return from a weekend with the guys to find your wife has painted the living room and purchased a new sofa.

**6** When your wife calls you by her old flame's name.

**7** When your wife says, "Let's put the kids to bed early tonight."

*Choose your next sentence carefully when your wife leaves the driver's seat in the forward position and you crack your kneecap.*

If You Are a Female...

**1** When your husband leaves the toilet seat up and you break the surface.

**2** When your husband spends more money than budgeted to buy a new computer gaming system.

**3** When your husband admits that he and his buddy already have tickets to the football game for that evening.

**4** When your husband asks you if your friends like him.

**5** When you return from a weekend at your sister's to find that your husband hasn't mowed the lawn or cleared the fast-food bags off the counter.

**6** When your husband calls you by his mother's name.

**7** When your husband says that he loves you and would marry you all over again.

*Think carefully before reacting when your husband indulges in activities you consider childish.*

# HOW TO IDENTIFY AN ILL SPOUSE

Traditional marriage vows used to promise "in sickness and in health." But to be a good spouse in times of sickness, you need to know when your loved one is ill. So here are some tips for how to identify an ill spouse.

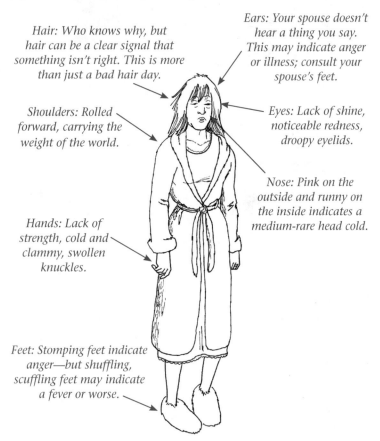

*Hair: Who knows why, but hair can be a clear signal that something isn't right. This is more than just a bad hair day.*

*Ears: Your spouse doesn't hear a thing you say. This may indicate anger or illness; consult your spouse's feet.*

*Shoulders: Rolled forward, carrying the weight of the world.*

*Eyes: Lack of shine, noticeable redness, droopy eyelids.*

*Nose: Pink on the outside and runny on the inside indicates a medium-rare head cold.*

*Hands: Lack of strength, cold and clammy, swollen knuckles.*

*Feet: Stomping feet indicate anger—but shuffling, scuffling feet may indicate a fever or worse.*

# FOUR BIBLICAL PASSAGES TO QUOTE WHEN YOU CALL YOUR SPOUSE BY AN OLD FLAME'S NAME

Some situations are too difficult for earthly solutions, so when you call your spouse by an old flame's name, try using the Word of God. Here are a few passages you could quote:

❶ "I am speaking as a fool" (2 Corinthians 11:21). But do not mix this verse up with 2 Corinthians 12:11: "I have been a fool! You forced me to it."

❷ "My mouth is dried up like a potsherd, and my tongue sticks to my jaws" (Psalm 22:15). Try to distract your spouse by explaining that a potsherd is a broken piece of pottery.

❸ "I will guard my ways that I may not sin with my tongue; I will keep a muzzle on my mouth" (Psalm 39:1). You may need to remind your spouse that we do not interpret this verse literally.

❹ "Do forgive my sin just this once, and pray to the LORD your God that at the least he remove this deadly thing from me" (Exodus 10:17). Asking forgiveness is better than trying to explain. Sackcloth, ashes, and groveling may be required.

# HOW TO MAKE YOUR MARRIAGE A SPRINGBOARD FOR MINISTRY

As you go about your daily lives, God can bless others and the world through you, through your spouse, and through the two of you together. Here's one way to launch your shared ministry.

**❶ Start with frank talk about how God has been speaking to you.**
This is a good indicator of where and what God is calling you to do. Try to develop a vocabulary of honesty with your spouse that gives you the freedom to express thoughts that are still in progress.

**❷ Dream together. Discuss. Repeat.**
The ability to articulate together what you think you hear from God goes a long way toward finding and doing those things. Take courage as you step forward in faith.

**❸ Pray together about what God is calling you to do.**
Do this every day. Repeated prayer draws you close while focusing together on God's word. Prayer is the single most effective strategy for developing a common desire for ministry.

**❹ Read together.**
Start with the Bible. Look for ways God blesses people through others. Put God's word into practice. Biographies and novels can also stimulate your spirit.

**⑤ Serve together using your spiritual gifts.**
Look for opportunities inside and outside the congregation. You'll be tempted to look only inside the church for ways and opportunities to serve. Resist! After all, the God of the universe intends to bless all people of the earth. So look all over the world for opportunities to bless and serve others.

*To begin thinking about your marriage as a springboard for ministry, read the Bible and look for ways God uses people to bless others and the world.*

# HOW TO USE YOUR SPIRITUAL GIFTS IN YOUR MARRIAGE

God gives spiritual gifts for the maturing of a congregation, but those same gifts can be used within a marriage. Using your spiritual gifts inside your marriage opens up opportunities to minister together, helps you learn how God works through your spouse, and points your whole family toward service.

**❶ Discern your spiritual gifts together.**
Your pastor or church office may have a spiritual-gifts inventory for you to use. If not, you can discover your spiritual gifts by trying different venues for serving God. You know you've found your spiritual gifts when you hear someone was helped by what you did.

**❷ Adjust your long-term direction as you learn how God has gifted you as a couple.**
For instance, if she has the gift of teaching and he has the gift of service, then together you might join a small group, where you both could use your gifts.

**❸ Use your gifts inside the marriage to honor and respect your spouse.**
People with the gifts of service are at a natural advantage in this, because they are fulfilled when helping someone else.

**4** Recognize that God uses your spouse.

This can be almost as thrilling as realizing that God is using you. When you see God working through your spouse, mention it.

**5** Employ the prophetic, truth-telling gift in marriage judiciously and with caution.

It's not that the truth shouldn't be told. It's just that it must always be done in love.

# HOW TO FORGE A STRONG SECOND MARRIAGE

Remarriage brings changes in legal, emotional, and financial issues. Although very complex and full of challenges, remarriage can be a wonderful new experience if you deal with the past by planning for future success.

**1** **Resolve issues with your first marriage through prayer, therapy, divorce recovery work, or visits with your pastor.**
If your marriage ended with divorce, assess and resolve your share of the responsibility, and address the personal problems that contributed to the marital distress.

**2** **Avoid paying the high cost of remarrying in haste.**
It's best to proceed with caution. You don't want to make the mistake of jumping into a second marriage too quickly without time for healing.

**3** **Remarry for the right reasons.**
It's better to remain single than to compromise your beliefs, values, and goals. Remarry because you've found someone you want to be with forever, someone you adore and who brings out the best in you.

**4** **Be prepared to make compromises.**
You bring habits from a previous marriage that your new spouse doesn't share. You'll need to work together to build new rituals and traditions that truly belong to the two of you.

**❺** Tell the truth about money.

Finances are complicated enough without entering into marriage with anything less than full disclosure. Focus on goals, dreams, and make sure you have a will.

## Please Note

- Consider a prenuptial agreement, which helps you identify the value of gifts and inheritances you receive, protects you from your partner's pre-marriage debt, and ensures that children from a prior marriage receive their intended inheritance.

*Your new spouse may not share your habits from a previous marriage. Learn the fine art of negotiating a compromise.*

# HOW TO PARENT YOUR SPOUSE'S CHILDREN

Being a stepparent isn't easy, but it's one of the most common major life adjustments in our society. And despite the challenges, being a stepparent can be very rewarding.

**❶ Take the time necessary to keep your marriage strong and loving.**
The success of a stepfamily depends on the quality of the marriage of the spouses who lead it.

**❷ Acknowledge that stepfamilies are different from traditional families.**
Children in stepfamilies represent a tangible link to a family that existed before the stepfamily. Former in-laws, ex-spouses, and former relatives are all a part of a stepfamily. Give them your respect.

**❸ Assure your spouse's children that you can never replace their biological parent and don't wish to do so.**
You have a special role as a mentor and a friend, but you are not the parent. Avoid putting the child in the position of having conflicting loyalties.

**❹ Avoid making decisions about your stepchildren's behavior.**
Although it's tempting, discipline of the children belongs to their parent, not their stepparent. Your role is to be supportive of your spouse as a parent. Conversations about discipline should be held in private, never in front of the children.

**❺** Model good morals and behavior for your stepchildren.

Let them see and know you are a person of integrity.

## Please Note

- Don't push for your spouse's children to call you Mom or Dad. They may eventually feel comfortable doing this, but leave it up to them.

- Allow your spouse to spend time with his or her children alone. Respect the time he or she needs to keep these relationships strong.

# Early Years

# HOW TO MANAGE A HOUSEHOLD CALENDAR

**❶** Start by choosing activities carefully and deliberately, with your priorities in mind.

- Does the activity conflict with Sunday worship?

- Does the activity conflict with family dinnertime?

- Is the activity beyond the income God has given you?

- What values are encouraged by this activity?

- What supervision and role models are provided during the activity?

- Would the activity be more beneficial if it waited a year?

- How would the activity affect everyone else's schedule?

**❷** Set up a large calendar in a central place for special one-time events, regular weekly activities, and each day's schedule.

- Retain school, church, and sports fliers and transfer dates every few days to the central calendar. (Time-saving tip: have a pen in hand when you read school newsletters and church bulletins. Mark dates and items to be transferred to your central calendar.)

- Consider making a grid for weekly music lessons, after-school activities, and regular church or club events. Use an adhesive note or an index card that can be attached to the main calendar.

- Add gym days ("Remember shoes"), band days ("Johnny—Tuba!"), and library days.

- Consider adopting this rule: "If it's not on the central calendar, it isn't happening."

## Please Note

- Daily reminders benefit everyone: Give a "traffic report" every evening and remind each person about the next day's activities, drop-offs, and pick-ups. If you share a car with a spouse or teen, review those arrangements the night before, too.

# HOW TO START AND MAINTAIN YOUR OWN HOLIDAY TRADITIONS

**❶ Reminisce about the past.**
Talk with each other about the traditions, foods, and activities important to making each holiday special to you. Recognize the emotions and memories attached to traditions and family activities.

**❷ Discuss expectations.**
Talk with your families about expectations for holidays now that you are married. Then talk with your spouse about the expectations you are willing to meet.

**❸ Focus on faith.**
Discuss how to include God's gifts at the center of your religious holiday traditions.

**❹ Consider your work schedules and finances.**
Your work schedules and finances will play a large role in holiday planning and traditions, limiting or opening up possibilities.

**❺ Start small.**
Your parents and families have had years to accumulate decorations and traditions. Do not pressure yourselves to have everything in order at the start of your marriage. Your collection of decorations and traditions will grow just as your relationship will grow.

**❻ Be honest about your decisions.**

Becoming a new family may require you to adapt or omit some previous family traditions. This can be difficult, but be sure to tell your families what you've decided.

*Don't forget to include inexpensive holiday traditions you both enjoy.*

**❼** Keep your options open for new traditions.
Throughout your marriage, continue to talk about how
you will celebrate upcoming holidays, especially when
there are changes in your lives or in your extended
families. After the birth of a child, a move across the
country, or a death in the family, you might change
some traditions or adopt new ones.

## Please Note

• Some of the most meaningful holiday traditions cost
  very little or nothing: worshiping together at a sunrise
  service on Easter morning, inviting someone who is
  alone to have Thanksgiving dinner with you, Christmas
  caroling in your neighborhood or at a long-term care
  center, or sharing a New Year's kiss with your spouse.

# HOW TO CHOOSE YOUR CHILD'S GODPARENTS

The following questions can help identify good candidates for godparenting.

**1** Do they believe in Jesus Christ?

**2** Are they baptized?

**3** Are they striving to actively participate in a relationship with God and a faith community?

**4** Can they openly share their faith and talk about how God is active in their lives?

**5** Can they keep their promises?
Godparents make promises to bring the child to worship, teach the Lord's Prayer, the Creeds, and the Ten Commandments. They promise to provide the Holy Scriptures with instruction (*Lutheran Book of Worship*, page 121). Have a conversation with candidates about what it would mean to keep these promises.

**6** Will they allow your child to ask questions about faith openly and honestly, without dismissing them or giving patronizing answers?

## Please Note

- It is common to choose best friends or family members as godparents, but choose such a person only if you can answer "yes" to the above questions.

- Pray and seek the guidance of the Holy Spirit when choosing godparents.

# HOW TO GET YOUR FAMILY TO CHURCH ON SUNDAY MORNING

Rounding up family members and moving them from home to pew requires different tools on different Sundays. Maintain flexibility in your struggle. Be proactive.

**1** **Shift into battle mode prior to Sunday morning.**
Obstacles may include Sunday morning cartoons, stubbornness, fatigue from Saturday evening activities, slow chewing at breakfast, and so on.

**2** **Approach the problem as a team whenever possible.**
In cases where two parents live in the household, both must support the decision to attend church regularly. Work it out together prior to Sunday morning. Remember, the family is not a democracy.

**3** **Make as many preparations as possible in advance.**
Pre-select church clothes after checking the next day's forecast. Include matching dress socks and clean underwear. Plan a quick breakfast. Set multiple alarm clocks equipped with battery backup in case of power outages.

**4** **Preempt stomachaches, headaches, and other "illnesses."**
If a miraculous recovery following church appears imminent, make it clear that whatever illness and subsequent treatment comes for the morning, stays through the day.

❺ Make church an ironclad routine.
"It's a church night," easily replaces, "It's a school night."

❻ Know the law: "Remember the Sabbath day, and keep it holy."
Relaxing, fishing, becoming one with nature, and washing the car do not count as keeping the Sabbath. It's a Commandment; look it up.

❼ Pray for help. Miracles do happen.

*Shift into Sunday morning mode on Saturday night.*

## Please Note

- If your family reports disliking church, attempt to discover why and make changes when feasible. Be ready to adjust your own attitude to boost church-attendance morale among your family members.

- Both parents attending church is the single largest indicator of whether a child will attend church in adulthood. (According to a recent study, when both parents attend church regularly, 72 percent of children continue in the faith. When only the father attends, that percentage drops to 55 percent. But when only the mother attends, just 15 percent of children remain involved in the church.)

- People who attend worship are more likely to volunteer their time to make a positive contribution to society.

- How you spend your time is a reflection of your values and beliefs. Actions speak louder than words. Get driving.

- Consider bathing small children on Saturday night to save time Sunday morning.

# HOW TO PACK A DIAPER BAG FOR WORSHIP

Many families with infants and toddlers place their children in the nursery during worship. There is great value, however, in introducing a child to the worship life of a congregation. A well-stocked diaper bag will equip you to anticipate and defuse challenges that arise during a typical worship service.

**❶ Be prepared for impromptu feedings.**
Keep a bottle with formula or breast milk ready. If nursing, decide on a location before the service where you will feel comfortable feeding your baby. Consider packing a light blanket for privacy, if you prefer, but try not to alter your baby's feeding schedule. Burp cloths will protect your clothes from spit up and other messes.

**❷ Choose snacks wisely.**
Make sure your child's snacks are not too loud, crunchy, sticky, or crumbly. Toasted oat cereal and fish crackers are time-tested and tasty. Tidy up any crumbs or drooly tidbits.

**❸ Select a variety of quiet toys.**
Soft toys, such as stuffed animals, cloth finger puppets, and board books are all appropriate alternatives (especially if they are biblically themed) to playthings that make music or other sounds.

**❹ Include diapers, wipes, a changing pad, and an extra outfit.**
Savvy caregivers prepare for unexpected eliminations of all types. Stay alert for any leaks or unusual smells.

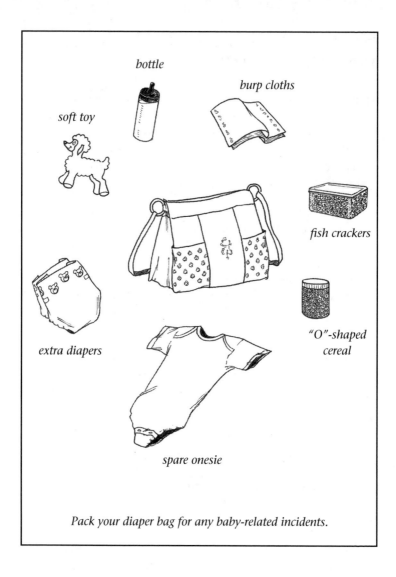

bottle

burp cloths

soft toy

fish crackers

extra diapers

"O"-shaped cereal

spare onesie

*Pack your diaper bag for any baby-related incidents.*

# Please Note

- You are more likely to pack a well-stocked bag when you prepare it the night before worship. As with all things, think ahead.

- Research has shown that young children are more likely to show interest in items when they are new. Toys that a child sees only once a week are more interesting than toys he or she plays with every day.

- Many churches worship at several different times on a Sunday. Choose a worship time that corresponds well with your child's feeding and sleeping schedule.

- If you forget your diaper bag or find that you are missing key supplies, DO NOT PANIC. Most church nurseries stock extra diapers and wipes. Additionally, offering envelopes and attendance cards can substitute as toys and occupy children of many ages. Beware of paper cuts.

# THE TOP FIVE CRITERIA FOR EVALUATING THE CHURCH NURSERY BEFORE PUTTING YOUR KIDS IN THERE

While some families choose to have their infants and toddlers accompany them to worship, the nursery is an important option for caregivers. Use the following criteria to assess a church nursery.

**❶ Overall nursery cleanliness.**
Make a cursory examination of the floors, walls, shelves, toys, play structures, and furniture. If it appears the nursery receives rare or inadequate cleaning, ask the pastor or person in charge of children's ministry for a copy of the schedule for vacuuming floors, cleaning walls and surfaces, and sanitizing toys.

**❷ Sturdy, sanitary diaper-changing station.**
This should be equipped with a safety belt to prevent the child from rolling off. Look for strategically placed antibacterial wipes or other cleaning products for sanitizing the changing surface after each use. Non-latex gloves should be provided.

**❸ Safe, clean toys.**

Some congregations accept all toy donations from members. While such generosity is well meant, this indiscriminate acceptance may lead to a sizable collection of broken, outdated, and unsafe toys. All toys should be in good condition and appropriate for all ages. Immediately report items that present a choking hazard. Goobers, boogers, crusties, and unidentifiable goo on toys should be thoroughly removed.

*Goo of any kind should be removed from church nursery toys with a safe germicidal solution.*

**❹** Established or posted policies for nursery staff and volunteers.
A church nursery should have two or more leaders in the room at all times. Paid staff in particular should undergo background checks and have certification in infant and child CPR and first aid. Inquire about expectations for parents who volunteer and make sure that an adult is always present when youth serve as nursery helpers.

**❺** Faith and fun.
A church nursery is an important context for faith formation of the church's youngest members. Toys, books, artwork, and staff attitudes should reflect a caring Christian environment. The nursery should also be a place where young children enjoy their time with nursery staff and other children.

## Please Note

• In many congregations, when members offer ideas about improving facilities, they often find themselves leading a committee to make the changes.

• Don't hesitate to ask questions about policies and priorities when it comes to the care of your child and other children, Jesus' littlest followers.

# HOW TO HANDLE YOUR CHILD'S NON-LUTHERAN FRIENDSHIPS

**❶ Allow your home to be THE place for existential conversations.**

That is, conversations about our existence. Engage your children and their friends in conversations about faith. Even young children are concerned with the meaning of life, death, and the future. Allow them to enter their teen years with a sense of freedom to approach you about their faith.

**❷ Be clear in your understanding of Christianity and Lutheranism.**

Consider purchasing a copy of *The Lutheran Handbook*. Do your best to understand the meaning of grace, infant baptism, the term "born again," and the importance of the sacraments.

**❸ Be prepared to respond to questions about your household's faith tradition.**

"Yes, we will attend the Ash Wednesday service because it is our time to remember our need for God's grace. Invite Jason to come with us." Or, "Haley is being baptized next Sunday. As Lutherans, we understand baptism to be God's action through water and the Word. It is a free gift for us. Ask Hannah to come with us."

## Please Note

• Peer groups have more influence on your children's thoughts and ideas by the time they reach preteen years. Lay the foundation early.

# HOW TO ADOPT A CHILD

**❶ Pray.**
Are you ready to make a lifetime commitment? Pray for discernment.

**❷ Identify what support is available to you.**
Support groups and secular or religious counseling are available to help you through the adoption process.

**❸ Do the research, learn the lingo.**
Attend a workshop conducted by an adoption agency. Learn the language of adoption. Read about the process.

**❹ Clarify your needs and wants.**
Are you interested in an infant, a toddler, or an older child? Will you consider an interracial adoption or a special needs child? Decide between a domestic and an international adoption. Choose between a public or private agency, such as Lutheran Social Services. Consider a "foster to adopt" program.

**❺ Work your resources.**
Adoption costs can range from very little to tens of thousands of dollars. How will you finance an adoption? Consult a tax attorney regarding current adoption tax laws.

**❻ Consult your calendar.**
Does your employer provide adoption leave? Some international adoptions require the adopting parents to travel to the foreign country or to live there while the adoption is finalized.

*Though often cumbersome, adoption agency paperwork is an important step in the process of adoption. To survive the ordeal, remain focused on the goal: loving and raising your adopted child.*

**❼ Complete paperwork.**
Complete the agency's application forms. Complete the home study (putting on paper intimate details about your childhood, significant relationships, marriage, and personality). Complete the background check, providing certified birth and marriage certificates and a criminal background check.

**❽ Use the waiting time productively.**
Pray for the child, the birthparents, the adoption workers, and yourselves. Assemble a welcome book or video about you to give to the child. In interracial and cross-cultural adoptions, read up on your child's history, traditions, and rituals. Prepare the home, perhaps outfitting the child's bedroom or, if the child is older, be ready to allow the child to make decisions about decor and furnishings.

**❾ Welcome the child.**
When the day arrives, have a "welcome home" party. Plan a ritual for welcoming the child into the family, offering thanksgiving to God.

**❿ Create the essential support network for yourself and your child.**
Locate a pediatrician. Add your child to your health benefits. Enroll your child in school or day care as needed. Secure an adoption therapist or other mental health professional for you and your child. Consult with a lawyer to update your will. Line up post-adoption support through a support group or counselor, and make arrangements for respite care.

# HOW TO FLOURISH IN A MARRIAGE WITHOUT CHILDREN

**❶ Actively avoid feelings of guilt or regret.**
No matter what others might say to you, a two-person family doesn't mean the marriage is fruitless. Consider what callings and vocations God may have for you beyond parenting.

**❷ Redirect parental instincts toward other healthy activities.**
Maternal and paternal impulses can be reshaped in order to nurture friendships, business relationships, work habits, and leadership identity. Avoid "parenting" your pets by putting booties and rain slickers on them.

**❸ Consider a vocation that nurtures children.**
Teaching provides an obvious opportunity to interact with children on a daily basis, but it's not the only option. Other positions—such as nursing, driving a school bus, coaching, and directing choirs—provide similar opportunities.

**❹ Involve yourself in mentorship activities.**
Mentoring, whether informally or through an organized program, offers a chance to interact one on one with someone who can benefit from your experience, helping him or her to grow.

**5** Volunteer your time outside the home; explore your spiritual gifts.

Opportunities abound—through schools, libraries, emergency respite, and more—to help, mentor, and encourage children.

**6** Support.

Attend performances, buy fundraiser items, and sponsor a child's dance/skip/walk-a-thon.

**7** Consider offering to care for other people's children. Occasionally.

Offer to baby-sit for an evening or a weekend. Both you and the children's parents will enjoy the time. Plus, knowing you can unload the kids back onto the parents will make the time more enjoyable.

# Middle Years

# HOW TO SURVIVE THE SEVEN-YEAR ITCH

After several years, marriage may feel predictable, making the innate human need for variety problematic. Either spouse may develop a desire for something new and exciting. If this desire is pursued outside the marriage, it could lead to infidelity.

**❶ Focus on maintaining appropriate boundaries.**
Protect yourself by avoiding situations or conversation with members of either sex that could be viewed as sexually compromising. Don't set yourself up.

**❷ Plan ahead to remain faithful.**
Eventually the opportunity will present itself. Persons who have rehearsed appropriate responses to tempting situations ahead of time tend to avoid compromising their integrity better than those who haven't.

**❸ Talk openly; avoid keeping your struggles secret from your spouse.**
Communicate with your spouse about your desires, temptations, and internal wranglings. Brainstorm ideas to rekindle a lukewarm marriage. Consider budgeting for a romantic getaway. Note: Certain issues are better left unmentioned, as they will only serve to hurt a spouse when there is no real gain to be made by bringing them up. Use discretion and caution. Avoid broaching hurtful subjects for the sole reason of lashing out.

**④** Nurture your marriage creatively. Devote time and money to the effort.

It takes two to tango and two to spice things up. What can you do to jazz up your marriage? Start dating again. Surprise each other with cards or little gifts. Take the initiative. It could be fun.

**⑤** When in doubt, seek the assistance of a trusted friend or marriage counselor.

Healthy marriages can often survive even the most damaging insults by starting anew with the help of a professional. When seeking advice from friends, choose people you know will be truly honest and whose moral fiber you know to be honorable.

## Please Note

- You may be more susceptible to the "itch" to explore intimate relationships outside of your marriage if there is a history of infidelity in either of your families. Consider marital counseling in these cases.

- The demands of daily life can be overwhelming. If you are responsible for the care of children or older family members, be sure to make time for your marriage. Your relationship needs it.

# HOW TO DATE YOUR SPOUSE AND KEEP THINGS SPICY

You will both change with each event and stage of life, so it's a good idea to keep dating throughout your marriage to help you stay connected and to continually deepen your intimate knowledge of each other.

**❶ Try new things together.**
Don't get stuck in a rut. Be creative. Seek out activities like ballroom dancing, or if that's too pedestrian, try skydiving. Develop mutual hobbies that stretch you outside your comfort zones and bond you together.

**❷ Spend time together. Consider scheduling this time in your daily planner and on the household calendar to raise it as a value for the whole family.**
Time for just the two of you is especially important if you have children or a hectic lifestyle. Consider kidnapping your spouse for an occasional bed-and-breakfast getaway. If that's not possible, remember: It's the time together, not the expense, that counts.

**❸ Leave love notes.**
Leave romantic notes or cards for each other in unexpected places, such as bureau drawers or in the car. If your spouse travels a lot, you can hide cards or other treats in a suitcase or briefcase. (Warning: Your spouse may reciprocate and, in the process, accidentally find items you thought were hidden.)

**➍ Keep a marriage journal.**

Write notes to each other in a daily journal. Get as romantic or as silly as you'd like. It's for your eyes only and will be a daily reminder of your love for each other. Keep the tone in this journal upbeat; solve problems face-to-face.

*Leaving romantic notes in unexpected places where your spouse can find them can help keep your marriage spicy.*

**❺** Laugh together as often as possible.

One benefit of marriage is your relationship's history. Over time you develop private jokes between the two of you. Celebrate these and spend time laughing together. Consider also creating an "insiders" language only the two of you understand. Avoid nauseating others with pet names and googly eyes.

## Please Note

- You can date your spouse every day by planning little surprises. Celebrating your love is a good reason to give your spouse a card or gift anytime.

- If you have children, maintaining a dating relationship may seem "icky" to them—and they may express this sentiment. All the more reason to do it.

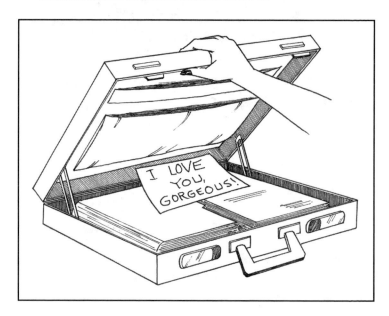

# HOW TO BALANCE WORK, HOME, AND CHURCH

Life is a juggling act. You and your spouse will have a variety of responsibilities. If you have children, demands upon your time will increase. This can be overwhelming, but intentionally structuring your time can help. Three areas to consider are work, home, and church.

*Don't drop the ball. Strive to balance work, home, and church.*

**❶ Maintain boundaries between work and home.**
Don't take work home with you on a regular basis, either on the physical level or the emotional level. This may be challenging, depending on the type of job that you have. It will be especially difficult if you run your own business. Leave family matters at home when you are at work, too.

**❷ Work with purpose.**
You will find fulfillment in your work if you have a sense of how you are making a difference in what you do. This is important in helping you maintain balance. If you are happy with work, it will be easier to live a balanced life with appropriate boundaries.

**❸ Schedule family time. Honor family time.**
Make spending time with your spouse and family a priority. Schedule dates together. Schedule a regular dinnertime and enforce compliance.

**❹ Take time to relax at home.**
Develop hobbies that permit you to forget about other concerns. Read. Learn to play an instrument. Do some gardening.

**❺ Make an accurate inventory of your gifts.**
When deciding what to get involved in at church, first think about your gifts and interests. Don't join the choir if you hate to sing.

# HOW TO PRESERVE YOUR MARRIAGE THROUGH YOUR KIDS' ADOLESCENT YEARS

Changes that affect one member of a family unit will affect the whole, resulting in a strain on your relationship with your spouse. Build a strong marital foundation from the start. Continue to work on your relationship and you will weather the storms of adolescent hormones.

*Together you can weather the storms caused by the presence of adolescent hormones.*

**❶ Maintain a united front.**
Communicate with your spouse on a regular basis about curfews, guidelines for use of the computer, and dating. Agree on repercussions if parental rules aren't followed. Be consistent.

**❷ Date your spouse. Attempt to generate a spirit of affection and playfulness in your marriage.**
Your adolescent may avoid you if you openly express affection for each other, granting you much needed one-on-one time. There are further benefits to this, as it may give you time to plot.

**❸ Seek mutual insights by troubleshooting adolescent incidents together.**
Dad may not understand why an otherwise polite and responsible daughter suddenly turns to crying and hysterics. Mom may be shocked and hurt if her son no longer wants to be seen in public with her and requests being dropped off a block from school. Seek insights and understanding from the spouse of the same sex as your adolescent. This may also deepen your relationship and awareness of each other.

**❹ Monitor the family stress level.**
If your family stress level gets too high, it will be more challenging to communicate in healthy ways. Remember that it is your job as parents to monitor family stressors and to provide a healthy steam valve when appropriate.

**❺ Hold regular family meetings.**
Adolescents have expanding interests and circles of friends. Meet regularly to discuss each person's schedule and how it affects the family as a whole.

**❻** Pray as a family.

Prayer can offer a spiritual foundation and give a calming effect on your life together. You and your spouse can also pray together. This will strengthen your relationship with each other and with God.

## Please Note

- Adolescents pay careful attention to how their parents communicate, even though they pretend not to care. How you navigate this time in your marriage may serve as a model for their lives.

- Hormonal changes in any member of the family can affect your marital relationship. This can also be true of "adolescence in reverse," also known as menopause.

# SIX TIPS FOR SURVIVING THE "SANDWICH GENERATION" YEARS

**❶ Embrace that hemmed-in feeling.**
It won't last forever, and thrashing around only makes it worse. You'll eventually become a slice of bread again.

**❷ Get sleep when you can, but accept the fact that your sleep is not a priority.**
Trust that you don't need as much as you think you do, but familiarize yourself with sleep deprivation and methods to combat it.

**❸ Devise and utilize effective methods for "disengaging" from the daily grind, even while still in it.**
Figure out what renews and re-juices you. Try to use time without family commitments as efficiently as you can. Learn to step away completely at least twice a day, so you can start fresh again.

**❹ Communicate often with relatives, professionals, friends, and God.**
Ask questions, express concerns, vent coherently, and share joys. Pray, alone or together, either with or without words.

**❺ Divide up tasks and delegate.**
Be honest with your spouse and siblings, if you have them. Some people prefer daily visits and soccer games; others prefer doing taxes and helping with homework. Keep everyone's blood pressure down by structuring real choices and sticking to them.

**❻** Openly embrace your function as the liaison between generations.

Introduce your kids and parents to one another's favorite music, art, food, and sports. Ask kids and parents open-ended questions within hearing distance of each other, and insist that they listen to the responses. Structure communication with e-mail, tape recordings, and phones until it becomes spontaneous.

## Please Note

- Don't try to fake it. You are modeling parent-care for your kids; your words, actions, and attitudes will come back to haunt you. Be caring and gracious, but also be honest. No one believes a perpetual smile.

*You may feel squished at times, but you can survive the "sandwich generation" years.*

# HOW TO HANDLE A CAREER CHANGE

Whether voluntary or involuntary, a career change is a time that can be daunting and challenging as well as exciting and invigorating—for the person making the change and his or her spouse.

❶ Take time to be together. Schedule this time in your daily planners and on the household calendar.
Pressures, including time and financial pressures, often increase. Spend time with your spouse and be sure to talk about all kinds of things, not just the career change or job search. Support each other and find ways to laugh together.

❷ Remain open to the invisible opportunities.
This is not just about you or your spouse "finding a job." Even if the career change begins involuntarily, start to think about this as a real opportunity for something new and exciting.

❸ Endeavor to persevere. Maintain as much of your routine as practicable.
If possible, remain in your present position while initiating plans for the career change. If you or your spouse loses a job, look for alternate ways to finance the career change, but keep the household on more or less the same schedule.

**❹** **Research your options together exhaustively.** Take advantage of the Internet to research "career change" and the new field. You'll also find other resources there, such as career counselors and support groups. Include your spouse.

*Be sure to spend time together when one of you is going through a career change.*

**⑤** Capitalize on all of your experience when seeking new employment. Assist your spouse in creating a full, positive inventory of his or her curriculum vitae.

Most jobs provide the opportunity to learn more than what appears in the original job description. Avocations and hobbies also provide experience that might be marketable.

**⑥** Go to school or become an apprentice. Support your spouse to remain open to this idea.

If you are considering a new career that's completely different from what you've done before, check out colleges and technical schools for new training. Note: some people require extra support in these efforts, especially if school was a less than positive experience the first time around.

## Please Note

- This can be a stressful time, especially if finances are tight or the search for a new position continues for many months. Check with a doctor if you notice signs of depression in yourself or in your spouse.

# HOW TO RECOGNIZE A MIDLIFE CRISIS

**❶ Making opulent purchases not in line with the person's taste or income.**
The midlevel accountant shows up for work with Armani shades, a 1963 Corvette, and that omnipresent bald spot hair-weaved into history.

**❷ Melodramatically embracing a trendy spiritual path.**
Midlife crises bring into high relief the lack of a spiritual anchor. Those in crisis may respond by attaching themselves to the latest motivational speaker, pop psychologist, or New Age mystic.

**❸ Abandoning their spouse for a trophy catch.**
Those with marital issues will often pursue "the prize" rather than meet problems head-on.

**❹ Suffering from mental disorders, both real and perceived.**
The pressures of midlife crises can bring on depressive, anxiety, and bipolar disorders. Hypochondriasis can also arise during this time.

**❺ Showing up at church after a prolonged absence.**
Of all the signs, this is the one that may positively point toward repentance, redemption, and hope. Beware of short-term attentions to the religious life.

## Please Note
- Help is available for mental disorders. Consult with your doctor to rule out other conditions and to obtain a referral, if necessary.

# HOW TO MAINTAIN YOUR MARRIAGE AS YOU AND YOUR SPOUSE CHANGE

Like a vehicle, a marriage requires maintenance if it is going to keep running. Of course, vehicles simply fall apart over the years, while marriage partners change in more interesting and challenging ways. The process isn't smooth or easy, but you vowed to make the journey (and any needed repairs) together. Here's how to minimize tensions and maximize rewards.

**❶ Monitor each other's health.**
Know the symptoms of depression, diabetes, heart attack, and stroke. Track checkups and be involved in lifestyle choices that affect the body, mind, and spirit.

**❷ Calmly imagine life without your mate.**
What would change in terms of day-to-day routines as well as the big-picture management of space, time, and money in the event of your spouse's death? Talk together about what would be hardest to adjust to and what you would miss.

**❸ Avoid ruts as a matter of course; remember always to try new things.**
This will mitigate the shock of larger, unplanned changes you cannot control. Strike a balance between comfort and creativity. Try new recipes and restaurants, purchase new linens or dishes, and conquer new technology together.

**❹** Be honest about your needs and take care of them. Sleep in a bed (or beds) that allow you to get the rest you need. Insist on balanced meals and healthful snacks. Schedule time for exercise.

**❺** Haul out and read aloud to each other the vows from your wedding ceremony.
Those words were carefully chosen, even if they sound a little dated.

**❻** Identify your sources of physical and emotional support.

**❼** Expect to change and be amazed at how much change actually occurs.
Embrace your roles as companion, sounding board, audience, and hand.

*Every marriage requires careful, loving maintenance to keep it running smoothly over time.*

# Later Years

# HOW TO SURVIVE AFTER YOUR KIDS LEAVE HOME

**❶ Reconnect with family and friends.**
Make dates with your spouse. You need to get to know each other all over again—this could take time. Form a book club with a group of your best friends and invite a few new folks you would like to know better.

**❷ Renew your passion for work.**
Discern whether you have extra time for work-related projects, now that you don't have to take off early to catch that soccer game. Bone up on work-related skills you have postponed for the last 20 years.

**❸ Consider involving yourself more deeply in community and church-related activities.**

**❹ Adopt new perspectives on your relationships with your kid(s).**
Kids react in different ways to being away from home. Some talk on the phone every day. Some come home every weekend. Some only talk when they have something to talk about and can easily stay away except on holidays. E-mail can be a terrific way to keep in touch, because each person can write or answer on his or her own time. Let kids take the lead here, and try not to compare notes with your neighbors.

**❺ Engage actively in self-care.**
Know that the feelings you are having are natural. Your life becomes dramatically different when your kids are not around. Take it slow.

## Please Note

- If you don't wait until your kids leave home to do some of the stuff mentioned above, your nest will seem less empty when they do fly away. Prepare ahead of time.

*Once the kids move out, consider using their empty room(s) as your new hobby workshop.*

# TEN WAYS TO DISLODGE YOUR ADULT CHILDREN FROM YOUR HOME

**❶ Explore definitions of the term "adult" with your kids.**
Casually broach the subject at dinner by cracking open a dictionary during the dessert course. Ask your audience which definition they most identify with.

**❷ Fill all available space with your possessions.**
Don't give up those hobbies that have taken over the "extra" bedrooms. Adjust the space, but not too much. The truly needy will agree to sleep among knitting needles and glue guns.

**❸ Delegate the household chores.**
Spell out responsibilities for help around the house so that no one has to listen to nagging. When you don't get cooperation and the clutter becomes unacceptable, introduce a chore chart complete with gold stars.

**❹ Make obvious and ham-handed attempts to help.**
You want your children to be successful—preferably somewhere other than your basement. Stack job and apartment search fliers on their beds and leave printouts from Internet searches scattered around the house.

**❺ Enlist the help of their friends.**
Acquaint yourself with your children's more independent friends and loudly inquire as to whether they could help model a more productive lifestyle for your kids. Do this often. When all else fails, display news of classmate accomplishments on the refrigerator.

**❻ Teach your kids the joy of basic, frugal, yet tasty cooking.**
Locate recipes for dishes your kids can't stomach and stock the refrigerator with the ingredients.

*To dislodge your adult children from your home, consider cooking foods they find repugnant.*

**❼** Consult with other parents in the same situation.
Exchange ideas and offer support. Accept the challenge
to be honest about your children's skills and "prospects."
Conspire to assist one another.

**❽** Control the calendar.
Discuss the inevitable dislodging process thoroughly and
create a timeline for severing. Mark important dates on
the household calendar in red, such as, "(CHILD) WILL HAVE
NEW JOB BY THIS DATE."

**❾** Maintain a tenuous peace.
Work out a calm and respectful way to live together, but
insist on teasing along with testing, laughing as well as
listening—in preparation for real life.

**❿** Think of it as a reboot.
Make sure that dislodging means sending them on to
somewhere and something with tools and confidence.
Secure your relationship by including in your cheerful
goodbye an invitation to return, for a visit.

## Please Note

- Computers are a two-edged electronic sword. Minimize
the game-playing. Lockable models are available.

- Know the signs of depression. For more information, talk
with your doctor or check reliable Web sites.

# HOW TO SPOIL GRANDCHILDREN ROTTEN

Grandparents tend to do well at spoiling grandchildren, but spoiling them *rotten* takes some extra effort.

**1** Give treats and gifts.

*Spoiling grandchildren might come naturally, but it takes concentrated effort to spoil them rotten.*

❷ Play age-appropriate games with your grandkids—and teach them how to beat their parents at these games.

❸ Take them on trips to the playground, the beach, amusement parks, campgrounds, and so on, or tell them about the best trips you've taken.

❹ Watch professional or local athletes with them and teach your grandkids the rudiments of sports and how to enjoy them.

❺ Tell them unforgettable stories about their parents.

❻ Make up bedtime stories that have your grandkids as the lead characters.

❼ Encourage them in their schoolwork, and teach them the lessons of life you've learned from experience.

❽ Tell them whenever you can, "Grandma/Grandpa loves you for who you are!"

❾ Remind them whenever you can, "What happens at Grandpa/Grandma's stays at Grandpa/Grandma's!"

❿ Teach them to remind their parents how many years are left before they can get their drivers' licenses.

⓫ Give more treats and gifts.

# HOW TO GRANDPARENT OTHER PEOPLE'S KIDS

You do not have to have grandchildren of your own to grandparent other people's kids. Talk to parents and their children in your neighborhood, local schools, and congregation, and you'll find many opportunities to be a grandparent if you wish.

**❶** Find out what kids are really interested in, ask questions, and let them talk as long as they want.

*One way to grandparent other people's kids is to make a child feel noticed.*

**❷** Do something silly and make a child laugh.

**❸** Write notes, letters, poems and prayers to young people.

**❹** Make a favorite food together. Pop popcorn or make pizza.

**❺** Share a unique hobby—anything from bowling to junk welding.

**❻** Create a book together, complete with words and illustrations.

**❼** Give away something inexpensive from your home, with a story to go with it.

**❽** Call a kid who is a sports fan in the middle of a game you know he or she is watching. Cheer, tease, ask questions, and do small talk on the phone.

**❾** Pray for the children and young people you know. Give thanks, tell God the truth, make intercession, and ask for many blessings on their behalf.

## Please Note

• Be sure parents are okay with you grandparenting their kids. Better yet, get acquainted with the parents. They might need a dear friend too.

# HOW TO SURVIVE YOUR SPOUSE'S RETIREMENT

For someone used to being a vital part of a work environment, suddenly facing days on end that offer reading the paper as the main activity can be difficult. In fact, illness and depression may follow. Living with someone facing retirement can be a challenge. Action to survive should be mutual.

**❶ Plan together for your spouse's retirement.**
The retiring spouse needs to move toward new and better activities to fill the days. Renew and reinvest in favorite old hobbies or start a new one. Schedule vacations one year in advance to create navigable milestones for the critical first year.

**❷ Keep busy with your own interests and your own circle of friends.**
A person adjusting to retirement does not necessarily need his or her hand held all the time. Be a good example of a vital lifestyle and let them move ahead on their own journey.

**❸ Travel together.**
Visit old friends. Discover new places. Get better acquainted with your own community. Sell some stock and take the trip you've always dreamed of.

**❹** Set a time each day to talk—not about the weather, but about real subjects.
Share feelings. Be open. Listen. Once a week, write a letter to each other about how you are feeling and read them aloud.

**❺** Avoid nagging.
Pointing out a spouse's faults, weaknesses, and failings may seem helpful, but it's mostly destructive. "Therefore encourage one another and build up each other, as indeed you are doing" (1 Thessalonians 5:11).

**❻** Find ways to laugh together every day.
Whether you rent old movies, read books together, or share the Sunday funnies, discover what makes both of you laugh.

**❼** "Be kind and compassionate to one another, forgiving each other, just as in Christ God forgave you" (Ephesians 4:32).
These are good words to follow throughout the entire marriage, especially in times of transition.

## Please Note

• Watch for signs of depression or illness. Get help. Professionals can play a vital role in this transition. A complete physical for both of you is a good start.

*Discover new places together, close to home or far away, to increase your chances for surviving your own or your spouse's retirement.*

# HOW TO RETIRE WITHOUT RUINING YOUR MARRIAGE

**1** Decide in advance how much togetherness you can handle and adapt as you go.
Try it out. Spend whole days together and see how it works, then adjust and use what you discover to plan for the days ahead.

**2** Balance time together with adequate time apart.
Maintain new and old activities (and their circle of friends) you can enjoy together and activities (and friends) you can enjoy separately.

**3** Ensure that both of you have access to transportation.
If you can afford it, two cars can be helpful, at least at first. Independence sometimes needs wheels.

**4** Develop new interests you both enjoy.
Avoid hanging around the house. Boredom aggravates unhealthy togetherness, but new, mutually satisfying activities are a boon.

**5** Celebrate each other's accomplishments—even the little ones.
Being appreciated and applauded by a loved one makes everything seem brighter.

**⑥** Intentionally develop spiritual tools that build the marriage: encouragement, prayer, and patience. Seek also the gifts of forgiveness and love. "Above all, maintain constant love for one another, for love covers a multitude of sins" (1 Peter 4:8).

## Please Note

- Although it may be helpful to spend time with couples who have made a successful move into retirement, models differ. There are no universal models or "right ways" of relating. Find what works for you and do that without guilt or apology.

# SEVEN REWARDING WAYS TO SPEND TIME AFTER RETIREMENT

The key is to understand that retirement is not just freedom *from* work, but freedom *for* something else. Consider these new life opportunities.

**❶ Plan and build a new life structure.**
   Just as life before retirement has a certain structure and routine to it, retirement also needs structure and routine to maintain feelings of purpose. Put this into place immediately upon retiring.

*Set aside more time with God in your new routine.*

**❷ Increase the time you spend with God and pursuing spiritual disciplines.**

Begin building your new routine by setting aside more time with God. A pastor or a spiritual director may be helpful in choosing what you will do with this time.

**❸ Volunteer your time to charitable organizations; be careful not to over-commit.**

Give more time to your community and to your congregation. Volunteer at a hospital, a food pantry or a shelter.

**❹ Spend more time with family. Be intentional about it.**

Date your spouse. Take your children to dinner. Offer to baby-sit your grandchildren. Take your whole family on a trip everyone will always remember.

**❺ Enrich yourself and challenge yourself to grow.**

Continue to learn and experience as you did during your career. Learn things that you had no time to learn in the past. Pursue both serious and frivolous subjects.

**❻ Travel as much as is practicable.**

As you have the resources, go to those places you have always wanted to visit. Foist your travel log and pictures upon your family like your grandparents or parents did on you. It's your turn.

**❼ Mentor the development of a younger person.**

Be a sounding board for someone in the field you worked in. Seek out persons who are in danger of making the mistakes you made and offer the benefit of your experience. Avoid overbearing codgerliness and cootism.

# HOW TO SUPPORT YOUR SPOUSE THROUGH A SERIOUS ILLNESS

**1** Make sure your support system is in order.
Arrange for people to lean on and people to help you with meals, household chores, and child care. Attend to your own health with a physical exam and conversation with your family physician.

**2** Let your spouse vent. Validate expressions of emotion; don't stifle them.
This encourages an ill person to share emotions of anger, frustration, and helplessness rather than retreat into isolation, which could compound the problem.

**3** Present options that will take your spouse's mind off the pain.
Find ways to encourage laughter. Even minimal exercise releases powerful pain-killing endorphins into the bloodstream. Meditation and prayer are shown to decrease anxiety and stress levels. Whenever possible, join your spouse in pain-relieving activities.

**4** Empathize—but don't treat your spouse with kid gloves.
It's a fine line, but make repeated attempts to understand what your spouse is going through without succumbing to constant coddling or over-pampering. Remain alert for hypochondriacal tendencies.

**❺** Pray together.

A new level of intimacy can be reached between husband, wife, and Jesus, even during an hour as dark as Gethsemane itself.

*When your spouse is seriously ill, the road to "Super Spouse" looks tempting, but find people to help you with meals, household chores, child care, and other responsibilities.*

# HOW TO HONOR YOUR SPOUSE'S MEMORY

As with other life issues, there is no formula for correct remembrance. Bereaved persons should unapologetically follow their hearts.

**1** Set up an Internet memorial log for friends and family to share memories and thoughts about your spouse.

**2** Design the obituary, eulogy, and funeral service to give thanks to God for the life and spiritual journey of your dear one.

**3** Use memorial gifts to support an organization or cause that was important to your loved one, if possible.

**4** Enjoy things that brought joy to your spouse. Stand in her flower garden and say her name aloud. Read the Bible he read—and any notes he wrote in the margins.

**5** Find a special place for tiny "treasures" he or she tucked away.
While going through closets, drawers, and desks, you may find love notes you wrote each other, a feather or shell you both found, a photo from the past, a vase from a trip together, or a child's drawing. Some of these could be framed or become centerpieces for your dining table or take turns sitting on your nightstand.

**❻** Tell stories about your spouse, look at pictures, show videos, and pray with your family and friends.

**❼** Trust God and continue to live, love, and laugh.

*To honor your spouse's memory, trust God and continue to live, love, and laugh.*

# HOW TO PLAN YOUR OWN FUNERAL

Planning your funeral will give you peace of mind and make a difficult time easier for your loved ones. Here's how:

**1** Settle on a funeral location.

**2** Determine which funeral home to use and set up a prepayment plan if possible.

**3** Choose a location for burial or for scattering of ashes.
In the event you choose cremation, declare the location and manner in which you wish your ashes to be scattered, buried, or displayed. Declare also who you want to perform the task.

**4** Pick some great hymns to be sung at the funeral service.
Choose hymns that define your personal theology and that describe your relationship with God.

**5** Select a few favorite Bible readings.
Choose readings that have special meaning for you.

**6** Choose special people to be pallbearers.

**7** Determine the lunch menu, if you wish.
This is an opportunity for you to help your bereaved affirm their continuing lives even as they mourn your loss. Consider including a food only you love as testimony to your uniqueness.

**8** Identify any other items you want included in the funeral or burial, such as military honors, bagpipes, and so on.

*Planning your own funeral may involve getting specific to avoid any posthumous confusion. When directing your survivors how and where you wish your ashes to be scattered, consider drawing a picture as a visual aid.*

**⑨** Document the decisions you've made carefully, and give copies to someone you trust.
Make sure your wishes are fully known by your loved ones. Your passing may create confusion and conflict, especially among siblings, that you can prevent with a few simple, definitive statements in writing.

## Please Note

- Meet with your pastor as needed throughout this planning process.

- Don't dwell on death after you've planned your funeral. Distribute your plan and enjoy the peace of mind you've earned.

# HOW TO LEAVE A LEGACY

A legacy is a tribute to the meaning of your life. The values that you hold as individuals and as a couple will inform decisions about the type of legacy you create. Consider leaving both a financial and a spiritual legacy. While leaving financial assets is admirable, the value of a spiritual legacy is priceless.

**❶ Financial legacies.**
- Estate planning: Talk to a lawyer or a financial advisor about the value of your material estate. Make sure you have a legal will, preferably prepared by an attorney.

- Charitable giving: Discuss with your spouse how much your estate should contribute to a favorite charity. There are several charitable living trusts you can establish, depending on your intentions. Seek the advice of a financial advisor or attorney.

**❷ Spiritual legacies.**
- Ethical wills: While a legal will makes provisions for passing on material wealth, an ethical will is a way for you to share your values and beliefs with another generation.

- Memoirs: Consider writing a memoir to share important stories and details of your life with your descendants. Community colleges and local adult education centers often offer courses in memoir writing.

- Electronic publishing: Create a family history that can be electronically memorialized. Search for companies, such as Making Everlasting Memories (www.mem.com). Produce your own electronic presentation and create a DVD. Include your music or your artwork if you have these talents.

## Please Note

- You can start creating your legacy at any stage in life. A good time to begin is when you undergo a major life transition, such as the birth of a child.

- A spiritual legacy doesn't need to be elaborate. Pass down family photos. Write letters to beloved family members to be given to them after your death.

# Money, Sex, & Other Fractious Issues

# HOW TO NAVIGATE AN INTERDENOMINATIONAL OR INTERFAITH MARRIAGE

So the love of your life is not Protestant or maybe not even a Christian. Think of your differences as a marvelous opportunity for growth rather than as an obstacle to be overcome.

**❶ Choose an appropriate starting place. Avoid making it confrontational.**

- Don't assume you know everything about your spouse's faith (or your own).

- Take the lead in speaking about your own faith tradition and listen to your spouse with an open mind and heart. List the three most important things about your own tradition and the three biggest questions you have about your partner's tradition.

- Revisit this conversation on a regular basis.

**❷ Avoid taking an adversarial position; also avoid copping out.**

- Avoid boycotting all religious services. Dealing with your differences in this way robs you of a faithful community.

- Avoid saying, "Let's not expose our kids to any religion so that they can decide for themselves when they grow up." You wouldn't hold back from teaching your children to read so that later in life they can choose books with an open mind!

❸ Be proactive in acquainting yourself with your spouse's tradition.
- Visit your spouse's congregation. Ask the worship leader to talk about what is central to that tradition.
- Read some of the key writings in your spouse's tradition. Your respect for the tradition might grow after immersion in these works.

❹ Develop a worship plan.
This plan should include where each of you will worship, and where kids, if any, will worship. You might all attend one church together. You might alternate weeks or attend separate services with mutual support.

## Please Note
- Take care not to confuse kids or put them in the middle of a strained situation. Their growth in the faith stands at the center of this whole adventure.

*Develop a plan and decide where each person will worship. This prevents kids from getting caught in the middle of a strained situation.*

# HOW TO GET YOUR SPOUSE TO ACCOMPANY YOU TO CHURCH

**❶ Talk openly with your spouse.**
Ask, "What makes you resist going to church?" and then listen. Perhaps it's "boring" or "cheesy" or "full of hypocrites." Maybe he or she "doesn't get anything out of it."

**❷ Express your own thoughts about why you attend worship.**
Tell your spouse why worship is important to you, in your own words. Avoid making it a sales pitch; simply express your thoughts and feelings.

**❸ Persevere in patience and prayer. Continue to practice your faith disciplines unabashedly.**
Just talking probably won't do it all, but in combination with your loving and faithful example, it may make a difference.

**❹ Disabuse yourself of the idea that it is your responsibility to bring your spouse to worship or to faith.**
You can plant the seed. It bears fruit through the work of the Holy Spirit, the Counselor, who calls your loved one to faith.

*Really listening is a more effective technique for getting a non-churchgoing spouse to worship than bribery, rewards, guilt trips, and "the whine."*

# HOW TO PLAN A LUTHERAN VACATION

Lutherans are blessed with a global church community, rich with diversity yet amazingly interconnected. Vacationing families can use this valuable network to plan fascinating, relaxing, uplifting, educational, and fun vacations.

**❶ Dream big.**
No matter where on earth you're interested in traveling, chances are you can integrate your faith journey and your geographic journey.

**❷ Connect with companion churches in other places.**
Your home congregation or geographic region may be in a companion relationship with a church in another part of the country or the world. Your pastor or denominational office can give you contact and cultural information. You may even be able to travel with a local delegation to visit a sister church.

**❸ Join a Lutheran travel group.**
Lutheran travel companies, colleges, musical groups, and service organizations sponsor package tours and cruises to many places. Check ads in church magazines or search travel Web sites about vacationing with a group of other Lutherans.

**❹ Tour church buildings.**
Many destinations feature guided tours of historically or architecturally significant chapels, cathedrals, and religious monuments.

**❺ Participate in worship wherever you go.**
Almost anywhere you go, there are Christians who would welcome your presence at worship. Lutherans are uniquely prepared to overcome language barriers in worship because of the universally familiar form of the liturgy.

**❻ Schedule a servant event.**
Dedicating a portion of your vacation to a servant project will make your trip more meaningful. Consider volunteering with local agencies or congregations.

**❼ Explore your heritage.**
Your faith experience can be profoundly enhanced when you visit important religious sites. Travel to biblical locations, tour sites important in Martin Luther's life, or visit your familial home countries and reconnect with the churches of your ancestors.

**❽ Spend time at church camps and retreat centers.**
Lutheran organizations operate retreat centers and outdoor ministry sites around the world. Reserve a room, cabin, or tent, and enjoy opportunities for rest, meditation, Bible study, and personal devotions.

**❾ Be prepared to sing.**
When Lutherans gather, whether at a worship service, around a campfire, or in the back of a tour bus, it is probable that they will break into song.

**❿ Be prepared to eat.**
Another common behavior for Lutherans around the world is the community meal. If your vacation includes any church-related experiences, it's likely you will be invited to share a breakfast, lunch, or dinner with the locals.

## Please Note

- Incorporating faith-encouraging experiences in family vacation plans can result in radical life-changing events, especially when visiting distant places and building relationships with other Christians around the world.

- Rest and recreation are not sins. Lutherans believe that it's good and healthy to enjoy life and to refresh the body and spirit.

# HOW TO RESOLVE MARITAL CONFLICT

Marriage counselors point to two prime causes for prolonged marital conflict: a breakdown in the ability to listen, and a compulsion to control a spouse's behavior or feelings. Marriages can often recover from or avoid damaging conflict, however, by following these steps.

**❶ Employ emotional "martial arts."**
This "emotional intelligence" is based on the martial arts principle that if a person comes at you swinging, you can flow with the force of the blow rather than resist it, to diffuse any damage to either person. Note: This is not impotent passivity. It is an active form of seeing the anger or resentment, making a quick judgment not to react to it, and instead staying calm, rooted, and centered.

**❷ Listen—deeply and empathetically—and respond with "I feel" statements.**
Hear your partner out. Completely. When he or she is finished talking, make sure you can repeat back what was just said with an emphasis on emotional content. ("You're mad because I left my dirty underwear on the living room floor again.") Then, respond in the way that will make your spouse the least defensive. ("I see what you mean, but I feel a bit beat up when you mention that the second I walk in from a hard day at work.")

**3** Understand the dimensions of conflict communication—physical space and voice tone and volume.

Sometimes there is no point to continuing a discussion, because one person's emotional temperature is too high. It is perfectly acceptable at this point to walk away, as long as you leave the door open to further discussion. Also, by regulating the volume of your voice and keeping your tone measured and calm, you will prevent the disagreement from escalating.

**4** Admit when you are wrong and make amends.

When you make amends, you must make a concerted effort not to repeat the same offending behaviors.

**5** Employ tension-breaking humor.

Laughter can defuse even the most tense moments, as long as you find the joke mutually funny. Direct any jokes or humorous jabs at yourself, not your spouse.

**6** See a marriage counselor, if needed.

Seek out counseling resources through your congregation or other couples who have weathered a marriage crisis. A prime consideration for picking a counselor is that the person must serve as a thoughtful, creative mediator.

# COMMON MARRIAGE "STRESSORS" AND HOW TO MANAGE THEM AS A TEAM

Stress will occur through all stages of life and marriage. Some stressors may be recurrent, others stage-specific.

**❶ Early years.**
- Negotiating boundaries: Discuss household responsibilities. As with many other marital issues there is no formula here; making it work is the object.

- Negotiating finances: If you establish joint accounts, decide who will balance them and who will pay the bills. Plan all major expenses together.

**❷ Middle years.**
- Adjusting to life's changes: It is unrealistic to expect your spouse to remain the same as the day you married. Seek each other's counsel when making decisions that will affect your life together and communicate continually.

- Parenting: Children require time, money, and attention. Develop mutual understandings of your role as parents and define expectations around discipline and rearing techniques.

**❸ Later years.**
- Retirement: If one or both spouses retire, the pattern of your daily living is going to change, and you may need to renegotiate expectations and responsibilities. Develop hobbies and activities that you can do alone and together. Do this prior to retirement.

- Saying goodbye to your partner: Discuss this critical topic with your spouse. Create both a will and a living will. Talk about preferred funeral practices. It may cause emotional discomfort, but this will aid your spouse at the time of your death.

*Learn to adjust to life's changes. It is unrealistic to expect your spouse to stay the same as the day you were married.*

# HOW TO TALK TO YOUR SPOUSE ABOUT MONEY

If there is tension in your financial life with your spouse, attack the problem with honesty and perseverance. Make sure you work toward a mutually satisfactory goal, not domination of the other person.

**❶ By yourself, write down answers to these questions:**
- On a continuum between "tight" and "loose" with money, where do you fall?
- In your humble opinion, how would your spouse rate you?

**❷ Begin to look at the spending continuum together.**
- Turn a piece of paper sideways and draw a horizontal line across the middle. Tape a dime on the left edge of the line (signifying, "can barely stand to part with a dime"). Draw a smiley face on the right edge of the line ("money is no object if it buys happiness").
- In the middle of your credit-card cycle, explain which edge is which and ask your spouse to put an X where you would land on the paper.
- Mention diplomatically that you'd love to know where your spouse sees himself or herself on the continuum.

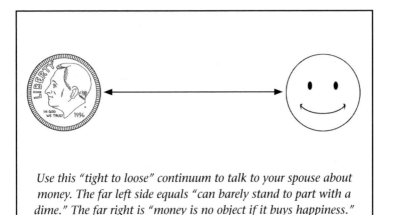

*Use this "tight to loose" continuum to talk to your spouse about money. The far left side equals "can barely stand to part with a dime." The far right is "money is no object if it buys happiness."*

❸ Compare your assessments of each other.
Suggest that these very traits are what attracted you to each other in the first place. Verbalize that you can get into trouble with your set of foibles.

❹ Shift the conversation to your life goals, both individually and jointly.
What do you most value in life? What do you hope for your future? How might your money life both facilitate and reflect this? Slowly shift from broad strokes to specifics and write these down.

**⑤** Think through ways you can structure your financial life so your shared values and needs get met.
If you spend like crazy, agree to an "allowance" every month. Commit not to spend more than this amount, and don't. If you are a tightwad, agree to let your freewheeling spouse retain complete control over a small amount, and do not feel resentful about or micromanage that money.

## Please Note

• If your spouse lands on the "money is no object" side of things and you fall on the other end of the spectrum, you could easily be seen as setting a trap, self-righteously plotting to shame him or her into compliance (and less spending).

# HOW TO WRITE A WILL (TO PREVENT A POSTHUMOUS FIGHT OVER YOUR ASSETS)

Think of writing a will as an extension of your love for your spouse and your family. Without one, the state will decide who gets your assets and the percentage they receive, which could cause financial hardship and stress for your spouse. Seek the counsel of an attorney familiar with the process.

**❶ Gather information and make decisions.**

- List your assets: This includes all personal possessions of value such as heirlooms, financial resources, and property.

- List your beneficiaries: List the family members, friends, and ministries you want to bequest with money or a specific item of importance.

- Select an executor: Think about who you want to oversee your estate after your death, which can be a time-consuming task. Your executor should be someone you trust.

- Make provisions for minors: Discuss and seek permission from a potential guardian for your children should you die before they reach adulthood. You will also need a guardian for their estate money. This need not be the same person.

- Consider establishing a trust if your estate is a large one: Your spouse and beneficiaries can receive income from your estate but will not have to pay taxes on the entire estate.

- Consider a Christian preamble: Check with your lawyer to see if this is possible.

**②** Contact your lawyer.
- Schedule an appointment: Speak with your attorney prior to your visit and see if there is additional information that you need to bring with you.

- Prepare questions: No question is too silly to ask.

**③** Work with your lawyer.
Your lawyer will help you turn your homework into a legal document that will fully represent your wishes after your death.

**④** Draw up a power of attorney.
This is a separate document that will allow someone to take care of your legal and financial affairs should you become incapacitated.

## Please Note

- Estate laws and the probate process vary from state to state. If you move, be sure to have a lawyer in your new state of residence check your will for compliance.

- There are resources to help you write your own will. Have an attorney review your will to be sure you have done what you intended to do.

- Your debts and taxes will be paid before your beneficiaries receive their inheritance. You can't escape taxes, even after death.

# HOW TO WRITE
# LIVING WILLS TOGETHER

Many people, when terminally ill, choose to refuse the efforts of modern medicine to keep them alive at any cost. A living will is a way to make sure those wishes are respected if the person becomes terminally ill and is unable to decide for him or herself. When spouses write living wills together, they have an opportunity to share their faith in God's promise of life in Christ as they entrust each other with their final wishes.

**❶ Read aloud and reflect on Romans 8:31–39 together.**
This passage reminds us that in all things God is with us. Not even death can separate us from God's love in Christ. Carry this faith into your discussions about living wills.

**❷ Obtain a copy of the living will form provided by your state.**
All states have a form. Study it together to make sure it says what you want it to say. You may feel that the standard form serves you well or you may wish to customize your living wills.

**❸ Make a decision on artificially supplied food and water.**
Living wills usually include a provision for whether or not you want to withdraw or withhold artificially supplied food and water, should you become permanently unconscious and the best medical judgment is that such food and water no longer

provides comfort or relieves pain. This is one of the most difficult decisions, so be clear with your spouse regarding your wishes in this matter.

**❹ Consult your physician.**
Your doctor can help you determine whether your living will provisions are as clear as possible. Your doctor also should know your wishes directly because it is very possible he or she will be attending you if and when the living will provisions become relevant.

**❺ Share your decisions on your living wills and what you intend with other members of the family and your pastor.**
The more caring people who know and understand your wishes, the better.

**❻ If, after consulting with your physician, family, and pastor, you have any concerns about the wording of your living wills, consult your attorney.**
You need only to have your living wills notarized upon completion.

## Please Note

• Remember that while Christians are committed to preserving life, they also know that death is not the end, but the beginning of a new and imperishable life. Read 1 Corinthians 15:51–58.

# HOW TO PLAN FOR RETIREMENT

**❶** Force yourselves to begin the process, regardless of your age.

This is the most important step of all. No more denial. No more excuses. Schedule an appointment with a financial advisor; ask about financial documents you might need with you and gather them ahead of time.

**❷** Make saving a value you hold dear. Cultivate an affinity for delayed gratification.

Start investing in your future by reserving money today. The younger, the better, but it's never too late. Research your options through your employer: IRAs, 401(k) and 403(b) plans, and other types of savings accounts and investment funds.

**❸** Dream together about your retirement years.

If you are under 50, this may be quite hazy, but it's a worthwhile exercise. You can make a good guess about your preferences decades from now. If you are over 50, things will start to come into more focus the older you get.

**❹** Work together as a couple and in partnership with your financial advisor to put real figures to your plans.

What kinds of retirement resources do you have? House? Retirement plan? 401(k) or 403(b)? Social Security? Cash-value life insurance? What kind of income will they produce in retirement?

**⑤ Align your income, your expenses, and your retirement plans.**

If resources fall short, you have three choices: save more, work longer, or live on less. That's pretty much it. If you have more than you thought, consider your options for philanthropy.

# HOW TO TALK TO YOUR SPOUSE ABOUT SEX

Open, frank, and loving conversation is essential to a mutually nurturing and satisfying sex life over a long-term marriage. Here are a few ideas that can help you with these important conversations.

**1** Nurture and maintain a sense of self.
"Differentiation" is the term psychologists use for the ability to maintain your sense of self in a relationship. Being your self—and being clear about your needs and desires (not expecting your spouse to read your mind)—is essential for healthy marriage and for satisfying sex.

**2** Sex is not a compartmentalized part of married life.
It permeates our lives. Often sexual encounters begin at the breakfast table with kind or anticipatory conversation. Sex might include a phone message during the day and a gracious word in the evening. Note: Sex may be contingent upon getting the dishes done or the countertop cleaned.

**3** Positive sex conversation starts at the beginning of a relationship.
Avoid entering your marriage with preconceived ideas of right or wrong sex, of what works or doesn't work. Make all expectations clear at the outset and negotiate compromise.

**④** Practice ASKING about your spouse's silent messages.
Assuming you can always interpret nonverbal messages
can lead to problems. Learn to listen to body movements,
pressures, and sounds. If you are not sure of the message,
ask. The momentary awkwardness is easily overcome,
whereas misinterpretation can wreck the mood.

**⑤** Speak in "I" statements; remain gracious and
affirming.
"I feel," "I understand," "I won't," "I think"— these are
"I" messages. This language avoids accusatory words,
such as, "You don't listen to me," "You don't understand
what I am feeling," and "You go too fast."

**⑥** Keep talking to work out your own particular
romantic vocabulary.
Making love in a marriage is an ongoing activity, not an
episodic one. It requires more than one conversation.
When dealing with something serious, consider
conversations with a specialist to help you get back
on track.

## Please Note

- The cultural emphasis on sex as personal fulfillment can
  be strongly at odds with the events and eventualities
  of actual married life, which involve large amounts of
  personal sacrifice.

- Some medications and diseases cause difficulties with
  sex. Be sure to talk to your doctor about any concerns.

- Married persons should always balance their own sexual
  needs against the greater good of the marriage.

# THE TOP FIVE WAYS TO STRENGTHEN MARITAL COMMUNICATION

In any relationship it is important to establish healthy communication patterns. You and your spouse will need to review your communication skills on a regular basis, as it is too easy to slip into methods that are ineffective.

❶ Cultivate an atmosphere of mutual respect.
Do not belittle your spouse in any way, ever. Do not share your spouse's confidential conversations with others. Use terms that communicate your respect for your spouse.

❷ Speak "I" to "I."
When expressing your opinion, use "I" language to state your feelings or observations. Encourage your spouse to do the same. This will get easier the more you practice it. Remember, you alone are in control of your feelings. Don't blame others for how you feel. Speak only for yourself.

❸ Plan time to talk and pray together.
Hectic lifestyles make it too easy to live a life on the run. Make time to talk and pray together each day. Consider mealtime or bedtime devotions as a healthy means to accomplishing this.

❹ Seek each other's counsel in weighty matters.
When making important decisions that will affect your life, speak with your spouse before you take action. What affects you will affect your spouse.

❺ Seek the underlying deeper meanings in what is said.

Ask your spouse for clarification on vague statements, without communicating judgment. Don't assume that you know what is intended.

## Please Note

- In the event you or your spouse experiences a sudden change of personality or communication style, see your medical doctor. Some illnesses can affect emotions and interactions with other people.

- Children will learn and benefit from the effort you put into developing healthy communication skills with your mate.

*When you marry, you do not suddenly become of one mind.*
*Don't expect to be in total agreement all the time.*

# THE TOP 10 IN-LAW ISSUES AND HOW TO DEAL WITH THEM

**❶ Conflicting political perspectives.**
Tread cautiously until you establish a firm, mutual understanding. Look for common ground and listen thoughtfully to understand where they're coming from. When you disagree, do so with respect.

**❷ "No one is good enough for my son/daughter."**
Rarely will anyone say this directly, unless they're uncouth in the extreme or are looking for open conflict. In the event such matters come up in conversation, respond with humor and humility, then quickly change the subject. Err toward taking the high road.

**❸ Widely differing communication styles.**
Some families trade spirited insults across the dinner table, while others sit in a silence rivaling that of birdwatchers. Study your in-law environment with care and venture a comment once you feel comfortable speaking the native language. Avoid boorishness, if that is your natural tendency.

**❹ The use of in-laws as convenient baby-sitters.**
In-laws who relish the grandma and grandpa roles will often appear anxious to relieve tired parents eager for a date night. But that doesn't mean their generosity should be taken as a blank check.

**❺ Extended visits from in-laws in your home.**
Close quarters can get tiresome, especially if you or your spouse will do the bulk of the shopping, cooking, and cleaning. Diplomatically make clear your expectations for the length of stay, and gently reinforce departure dates in conversation if necessary.

**❻ Extended visits with in-laws in their home.**
Be clear about the length of your stay and your departure date. Consider crafting a backup plan for early departure, should the situation become onerous. Make every effort to be a gracious, helpful houseguest during your stay.

**❼ In-law rants.**
Keep in mind that a rant is caused by emotion, so there's no point in engaging the debate intellectually. If it's after a big dinner, you could excuse yourself and go to the bathroom, where you may stay until the rant subsides.

**❽ Bad manners.**
Discuss the situation with your spouse first, then politely and diplomatically address the situation with your in-laws in tandem with your spouse. Expect it to feel awkward. Spousal agreement is critical. Do not proceed without it.

**❾ Extreme dissociative feelings (feeling like you're not part of the family).**
Only time can heal this issue; assimilation depends upon the host family's receptivity as an aggregate whole. Avoid forcing a solution. Maintain good humor and document odd behavior to reveal at a future family event, once you're on good terms.

**⑩ No common ground with your in-laws.**
Traditionally it is incumbent upon the new family
member to bridge the gaps, but trying too hard can
backfire. In cases where your new in-laws act graciously
to include you, be extremely grateful.

*In-laws sometimes rant. Simply allow the rant to pass
and the in-law will likely return to normalcy momentarily.*

# HOW TO BE GRACIOUS TO YOUR SPOUSE'S FRIENDS ...

| *Type of Friend* | *Irritating Behavior* |
|---|---|
| The Needy Friend | May call or show up at any hour and demand your spouse's attention. |
| The Childhood Pal | Spends hours reliving events that you were not a part of. |
| The Work Pal | Keeps your spouse at work. |
| The Possessive Friend | Tries to monopolize your spouse and exclude you. |
| The Hypochondriac | Always contracting a new terminal illness or deadly allergy. |

# EVEN WHEN YOU DON'T REALLY LIKE THEM

| *Coping Strategies* |
| --- |
| Get caller ID; remind yourself to be nice, since the needy friend makes you look good; avoid looking at your watch too often. |
| Try to redirect the friend's conversation to what he or she is doing in the present; avoid ridiculing this friend. |
| Try to invite the friend into other parts of your life; avoid sending your spouse on a guilt trip. |
| Express how glad you are that your spouse has such a good friend; make certain the friend knows how much you love and value your spouse; avoid throwing elbows. |
| Avoid trying to diagnose or treat the illness—this is what the hypochondriac wants you to do, and it only encourages him or her; realize that if this friend drives you to prayer, he or she is also driving you closer to God. |

| Type of Friend | Irritating Behavior |
|---|---|
| The Deadbeat | Being irritating is the only initiative they show. |

*Make repeated attempts to engage your spouse's Childhood Pal in conversation about the present.*

| | |
|---|---|
| **Coping Strategies** | |
| | Invite the deadbeat to help you with projects, big or small; avoid asking about the treadmill in his or her basement. |

# HOW TO AVOID BEING TRIANGULATED BY THE KIDS

Triangulation is classically defined as the attempt of one person (e.g., a petulant child) to communicate indirectly with a second person (mean old dad or mom) by going to a third person (peace-keeping mom or dad). Children are often expert practitioners of this subtle psychological interplay. Consider the following to avoid it.

*Children are experts at triangulation. The key is to stay in touch with your spouse regarding all questionable decisions.*

**❶ Remain mindful of triangulation's purpose and good parenting philosophy.**
The purpose of triangulation is to achieve the child's utmost immediate desire. The purpose of parenting, however, needs to stay consistent: letting children know that they don't decide what's good for them, you do.

**❷ Prepare ahead of time for triangulation attempts and strategize several response methods.**
Triangulation is not merely a possibility; it is part of the territory in child-rearing. Would-be parents should prepare for it during dating by discussing all aspects of raising a child.

**❸ Maintain a united front.**
Triangulation is discouraged when parents are perceived as always being of one mind. Keep a ready supply of stock phrases handy such as "Ask your mother" or "What did your father say about it?"

**❹ When in doubt, consult with your spouse.**
Not every attempt at triangulation, nor every request from a child, needs to be met with an immediate affirmative or negative response. Claim the parental right of time out to consult with your spouse.

**❺ Avoid making knee-jerk, unilateral decisions.**
Forgetting principles 3 and 4 above will lead to unilateral decisions by one parent, resulting in spousal wrath. After spending the night alone on the couch reviewing the above principles, schedule a marriage counseling appointment to save your marriage and avoid making this mistake again.

# HOW TO DECIDE WHO DOES WHAT AROUND THE HOUSE

Household chore delegation can be an area of contention, especially if no one does anything. To reduce frustration levels and maximize your effectiveness as a couple, sit together to discuss who will do what.

**❶ Write down a list of all known responsibilities.**
The list may include grocery shopping, cooking, washing the car, mowing the lawn, sweeping, mopping, vacuuming, dusting, doing the laundry, folding and putting away laundry, spring cleaning, taking care of pets, cleaning bathrooms, taking out the trash, and recycling.

**❷ Identify what you cannot do.**
Due to physical limitations, there may be tasks you or your spouse cannot effectively carry out (for example, lawn care or heavy lifting or, in cases where children are present, vomit clean-up duty).

**❸ Identify what you like to do.**
If you or your partner particularly enjoys a certain task, volunteer for it gladly. In cases where both partners prefer the job in question, take turns.

**❹ Split the remainder of the responsibilities equally. Factor in levels of difficulty and time duration.**
Divide up the responsibilities that do not fall in the "cannot do" or "like to do" categories. Divide them on a long-term basis, on a weekly basis, or on a nightly basis—or draw them from a hat, draw straws, or take turns. Carry out felicitous chores together.

**❺** Apply and adhere to the rules of fair play. Consider choosing one chore per day that belongs to your spouse and doing it for him or her. Helping your spouse in times of extra stress or as an act of kindness can help foster a sense of teamwork and love.

## Please Note

- "I can't do it—I don't know how," is not a reason to dismiss a task. Each of you should strive to learn new areas of responsibility around the home throughout your marriage. This will help when your spouse is ill or if you have children. It also wards off resentment.

- If you are very particular about carrying out a task in a specific way and your spouse does not meet your expectations, add that task to your list—or learn to be okay with the way your spouse does it.

- Re-evaluate responsibilities periodically to make sure both of you are agreeable to your tasks.

*Expedite a household chore neither of you wants to do by doing it together.*

# HOW TO SHARE THE TV REMOTE CONTROL

Dominating control of the TV remote can be very dangerous in a marriage. Adopt the following strategies to keep everyone safe and provide equal viewing opportunity.

**❶ The favorite list.**
Create a list that maximizes viewing of each spouse's favorite programs. Respectfully follow the list on a weekly basis, or until a new season begins. Use the TV listings in your newspaper or other publications to plan ahead.

**❷ Free trade agreement.**
Trade off control of the remote daily if the favorite list strategy cannot be employed.

**❸ The 20-flip limit.**
If you and your spouse have not chosen a particular program during a time slot, the person in possession of the remote makes a selection. After 20 "flips," this person must make a decision or forfeit the right to choose.

**❹ The commercial covenant.**
Do not flip channels during commercials without a mutual agreement. If there is no agreement, use the following to make commercials more enjoyable and less tantalizing to flip through: tell funny stories, eat something yummy, or cuddle.

**❺ The second set.**

Install another TV elsewhere in your home. Make sure the screen has smaller dimensions than the main set, to encourage togetherness.

*Tell funny stories, eat something yummy, or cuddle during commercials. This strategy significantly reduces incidences of channel-flipping.*